More Praise for *Hybrid Church*

"In the polarizing either/or debate between microchurch and megachurch Dave Browning inserts a convincing argument for both/and. As always Dave's view is engaging, challenging, and somewhat controversial; and in the end a viewpoint that anyone serious about ecclesiology in the twenty-first century should consider."

—Geoff Surratt, pastor of ministries, Seacoast Church, and coauthor, *The Multi-Site Church Revolution*

"This important book explains why healthy churches are getting smaller and larger at the same time. It argues that the preferred church design combines the intimacy of a microchurch with the impact of a megachurch, giving God's people the best of both worlds. This 'hybrid church' is no idle theory. It works itself out powerfully at Dave Browning's church—and it just might become the approach for your church as well."

—Warren Bird, Ph.D., coauthor of twenty-three books including *Viral Churches* and *Culture Shift*

"Most people can only find 'balance' in mediocrity. Others only experience it for brief moments, moving from one extreme to the other. Dave's contention is that genuine balance can be found by actually targeting two extremes, both at the same time. This book shows how both intimacy and impact are within all of our reach. If Dave is right, then the ongoing battle for legitimacy between megachurches and microchurches can finally end. Impact and intimacy—throw in détente and you've got *Hybrid Church*. It's about time."

—Tom Mercer, senior pastor, High Desert Church, and author, *Oikos: Your World, Delivered*

"Dave Browning is standing in the middle of the tension and the dream of every church. 'Mega' churches love the impact they are having in their community but will readily admit that their greatest struggle is achieving intimacy within their Body. 'Micro' churches thrive on the intimacy of their fellowship but are challenged to have a lasting impact within their community. Dave has been placed in the unique position of having credibility with both groups. *Hybrid Church* is a constructive dialogue between *both* models that promotes a novel idea—we can learn from each other—we *need* each other. This is a must-read for pastors and people who are living both sides of the same dream."

—Grant Fishbook, lead pastor, Christ the King
Community Church, Bellingham, Washington

"Dave tracks two of the rising trends in evangelicalism—the megachurch and the microchurch—and shows how they not only can coexist, but cooperate. Regardless of the size of one's ministry, any church leader can benefit from the collaborative concepts found in *Hybrid Church*."

—Dr. Charles Arn, president,
Church Growth, Inc., Pasadena, California

Hybrid Church

The Fusion of Intimacy and Impact

Dave Browning

A Leadership Network Publication

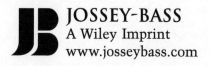

JOSSEY-BASS
A Wiley Imprint
www.josseybass.com

Published by Jossey-Bass
A Wiley Imprint
989 Market Street, San Francisco, CA 94103-1741—www.josseybass.com

Jossey-Bass books and products are available through most bookstores. To contact Jossey-Bass directly call our Customer Care Department within the U.S. at 800-956-7739, outside the U.S. at 317-572-3986, or fax 317-572-4002.

Scriptures taken from the Holy Bible, New International Version®, NIV®. Copyright © 1973, 1978, 1984 by Biblica, Inc.™ Used by permission of Zondervan. All rights reserved worldwide. www.zondervan.com

Jossey-Bass also publishes its books in a variety of electronic formats. Some content that appears in print may not be available in electronic books.

Library of Congress Cataloging-in-Publication Data

Browning, David, date
   Hybrid church : the fusion of intimacy and impact / Dave Browning. — 1st ed.
      p. cm. — (Leadership Network titles)
   Includes bibliographical references and index.
   ISBN 978-0-470-57230-6 (cloth); 978-0-470-88079-1 (ebk);
   978-0-470-88080-7 (ebk); 978-0-470-88081-4 (ebk)
  1. Church development, New.   2. Church growth.   3. Church renewal.
4. Small churches.   5. Big churches.   I. Title.
   BV652.24.B77 2010
   254'.5—dc22   2010018790

Printed in the United States of America
FIRST EDITION
HB Printing   10 9 8 7 6 5 4 3 2 1

Leadership Network Titles

The Blogging Church: Sharing the Story of Your Church Through Blogs, Brian Bailey and Terry Storch

Church Turned Inside Out: A Guide for Designers, Refiners, and Re-Aligners, Linda Bergquist and Allan Karr

Leading from the Second Chair: Serving Your Church, Fulfilling Your Role, and Realizing Your Dreams, Mike Bonem and Roger Patterson

Hybrid Church: The Fusion of Intimacy and Impact, Dave Browning

The Way of Jesus: A Journey of Freedom for Pilgrims and Wanderers, Jonathan S. Campbell with Jennifer Campbell

Cracking Your Church's Culture Code: Seven Keys to Unleashing Vision and Inspiration, Samuel R. Chand

Leading the Team-Based Church: How Pastors and Church Staffs Can Grow Together into a Powerful Fellowship of Leaders, George Cladis

Organic Church: Growing Faith Where Life Happens, Neil Cole

Church 3.0: Upgrades for the Future of the Church, Neil Cole

Off-Road Disciplines: Spiritual Adventures of Missional Leaders, Earl Creps

Reverse Mentoring: How Young Leaders Can Transform the Church and Why We Should Let Them, Earl Creps

Building a Healthy Multi-Ethnic Church: Mandate, Commitments, and Practices of a Diverse Congregation, Mark DeYmaz

Leading Congregational Change Workbook, James H. Furr, Mike Bonem, and Jim Herrington

The Tangible Kingdom: Creating Incarnational Community, Hugh Halter and Matt Smay

Baby Boomers and Beyond: Tapping the Ministry Talents and Passions of Adults over Fifty, Amy Hanson

Leading Congregational Change: A Practical Guide for the Transformational Journey, Jim Herrington, Mike Bonem, and James H. Furr

Contents

Dedicated to my pastors over the years who have "walked the talk":
Paul Weimer, Ludwig Zerbe, Ralph Colas, Gerald Zordel,
Bernie Augsburger, Fred Davison, John Ruhlman, Steve Mason.
Thank you. "Remember your leaders, who spoke the word of
God to you. Consider the outcome of their way of life
and imitate their faith" (Hebrews 13:7).

List of Tables and Figures

About Leadership Network

Leadership Network, an initiative of OneHundredX, exists to honor God and serve others by investing in innovative church leaders who impact the Kingdom immeasurably.

Since 1984, Leadership Network has brought together exceptional leaders, who are focused on similar ministry initiatives, to accelerate their impact. The ensuing collaboration—often across denominational lines—provides a strong base from which individual leaders can better analyze and refine their individual strategies. Creating an environment for collaborative discovery, dialogue, and sharing encourages leaders to extend their own innovations and ideas. Leadership Network further enhances this process through the development and distribution of highly targeted ministry tools and resources—including video, podcasts, concept papers, special research reports, e-publications, and books like this one.

With Leadership Network's assistance, today's Christian leaders are energized, equipped, inspired—and better able to multiply their own dynamic Kingdom-building initiatives.

In 1996 Leadership Network partnered with Jossey-Bass, a Wiley Imprint, to develop a series of creative books that would provide thought leadership to innovators in church ministry. Leadership Network Publications present thoroughly researched and innovative concepts from leading thinkers, practitioners, and pioneering churches. The series collectively draws from a wide range of disciplines, with individual titles providing perspective on one or more of five primary areas:

- Enabling effective leadership
- Encouraging life-changing service
- Building authentic community
- Creating Kingdom-centered impact
- Engaging cultural and demographic realities

For additional information on the mission or activities of Leadership Network, please contact:

Leadership Network
2626 Cole Avenue, Suite 900
Dallas, Texas 75204
800-765-5323
www.leadnet.org
client.care@leadnet.org

Preface

At a conference I attended, the facilitator said, "It's more important to be kind than to be right." At first the statement resonated with me. I've certainly seen rightness expressed at the expense of kindness. But upon further reflection, I think it was unfortunate that the conversation was being framed in terms of kindness versus rightness. Can't we have both? I think a better statement would have been "It is important to be right. It is just as important to be kind."

It's okay to be extreme, but it's not okay to be imbalanced. It was said of Abraham Lincoln that he was "a man of steel and velvet," extremely strong at the core, with a very gentle exterior. It was said of Christ that He was "full of grace and truth," completely truthful, but gracious. That is what I want to be when I grow up—both. And that is God's dream for all of us in His church—that when we grow up we will "speak the truth in love" (Ephesians 4:7–16). Greatness appears to be balanced extremes.

Balance is not very sexy or cool. What is deemed newsworthy is often excessive in one direction or another. The media tend to amplify the highly unlikely outliers and minimize the more commonplace "midliers." This is true in Christianity as well. The ministry that is extremely (fill in the blank: *large, evangelistic, Calvinistic, dogmatic,* and so on) gets noticed. But for long-term effectiveness, balance yields the best results, in your personal life and in your ministry.

A wise older pastor advised me in my youth, "Lean against the prevailing wind." He had used this phrase as a sextant for his personal life, his leadership, and his teaching. "If you find your-self preaching about grace all the time," he counseled, "maybe balance that with a message on holiness. If you've focused for a while on outreach, teach on discipleship." So much of spiritual-ity, he told me, is both/and, not either/or.

This book is about *both* instead of *either*, about *and* instead of *or*. Its focus is what is right with the church, from pole to pole—from the biggest, most impacting megachurch to the smallest, most relational microchurch. But instead of taking you toward one pole or the other, this book will lead you on an expedition to both extremes simultaneously.

My hope is that the book's tone will be conciliatory. Before my first book, *Deliberate Simplicity*, was published, I was told that the publisher liked its tone. The publisher felt that the book was gracious toward the traditional church even while drawing con-trasts with it. I was happy to hear this. In the foreword to that book, I wrote: "God is at work in every church, and in every church tradition there are elements that work well for the peo-ple in those traditions. We all have to be faithful to what God is calling us to be and do." I still feel this way. My prayer would be that this book will become known not just for the ideas pre-sented here but also for the manner in which they are presented.

We are called to experience and express the grace of God. There is no question that we have experienced grace. The ques-tion is, will we express it? And we need to extend grace in matters of style as well as in matters of sin. The church that I pastor, Christ the King Community Church, has become noted for being a place of grace for sinners. We tell you, without reser-vation, "There is always a place for you." We don't care where you've been or what you've done; we say, "God will take you where you are, He just won't leave you there." We believe there is forgiveness for the past and hope for the future. There is no question about how we feel about sinners. We love them, and love covers a multitude of sins. The question is, will we extend the same kind of grace to someone who differs from us in style? In other words, will love also cover a multitude of styles?

Thomas Jefferson put it so well when he said, "In matters of style, swim with the current; in matters of principle, stand like a rock." This has proved to be a difficult balance for Christians to maintain. We have tended first to gravitate toward certain styles (in preaching, music, liturgy, programming), and then to imagine that our preferred methodology must be "right," and then to become cynical, critical, or judgmental of others for being different. We imagine that the way God is at work in our story is the only way God could ever be at work. And in our efforts to validate our own method of ministry there is often a temptation to invalidate another's. We must resist this temptation. As Jefferson noted, style is an area where we want to see diversity, not unity. We want to be loyal to Master and mission, not to method and manner.

I have found that many believers have a wrong notion about Christian unity. We confuse unity with uniformity. Uniformity involves looking for little things we have in common with others, creating a group around those commonalities, drawing distinctions between the newly created group and others who do not share these points of affinity with us, and then increasingly insisting that others be like us in order to be in our company. But that is not creating Christian unity. That is creating worldly uniformity. And, frankly, anyone can do it, which is why everyone *is* doing it. But Christian unity means embracing diversity within the will of God (see 1 Corinthians:12). Do you see the difference? Within God's will there is grace for differences in personality and presentation.

Can you appreciate a sermon that is preached in a style different from the one you prefer? Can you worship with a song that isn't your favorite? Can you talk up a denomination that isn't yours? If not, you may need to take some of the grace that you have for sin and apply it to style.

It's a shame that the different wings of the church often look askance at one another. Imbalanced perspectives about ministry size have proved particularly corrosive to unity. Small churches tend to invalidate larger ones, and vice versa. As

G. K. Chesterton has noted, this imbalance is based on the phenomenon of "knowing what you know" and being far too confident about the rest: "If a man lives alone in a straw hut in the middle of Tibet, he may be told that he is living in the Chinese Empire; and the Chinese Empire is certainly a splendid and spacious and impressive thing. Or alternatively he may be told that he is living in the British Empire, and be duly impressed. But the curious thing is that in certain mental states he can feel much more certain about the Chinese Empire that he cannot see than about the straw hut that he can see."[1]

If we would come out of the bunkers that we have created with our mission statements and philosophies of ministry, we might find that there is something to be learned from our brothers and sisters who do things differently. In this book I contend that God works in different ways at different times and places. Rick Warren likes to say that he's neither right wing nor left wing but "for the whole bird." When a congregation stretches its wings toward intimacy and impact, it experiences greater lift.

This is a book about the church having its cake and eating it, too. I hope you don't believe the extremists who say, "You have to pick your poison as a church. You either are going to be big and impacting or small and intimate." Or if you do believe that, I hope you won't still believe it after reading this book. If you are tempted to buy into that either/or thinking, this book will point you in the direction of a beautiful blend. You don't have to choose. In fact, you don't *want* to choose. Both perspectives are critical. You should value both. You should pursue both. You need both. You should enjoy both. This is a book about having the best of both worlds, in a hybrid church.

August 2010

Acknowledgments

Many mentors have steered me over the years. I want to acknowledge a few whose direction is embedded in *Hybrid Church*.

Dr. Jerry Prevo is the longtime pastor of the Anchorage Baptist Temple (ABT). I never got to know him personally, but ABT was the first megachurch I ever noticed as a kid growing up in Anchorage, Alaska, and it made me want every church to be noticed. As a young man, I was greatly impressed by the magnitude of the ministry. A fleet of buses picked children up from around the city. A choir that was bigger than most other churches backed up the singing. Thousands of people were in engaged in dozens of ministries. ABT operated a Christian school (I was a student there for a few years). ABT was on television and on the radio. It was a big church that did things in a big way. That church significantly expanded the horizons of my thinking about what was possible for the church.

At the other end of the spectrum, in terms of scale but not significance, is Phil Ellis. Phil led the first small group in which I ever participated, a men's recovery group in which I experienced a fair amount of personal healing. Phil led me on my first foray into vulnerability. I experienced things in that group that are still reverberating in me today. Phil was particularly transparent, and he engendered the sort of safe environment in which we would all want to grow.

I made my first pilgrimage to Willow Creek in the early 1990s. What I remember, more than Willow Creek's mall-like campus, complete with a food court, was Bill Hybels and his unparalleled heart for people. Bill's passion for lost people blew away my skeptical stereotypes about what made megachurch leaders tick.

A one-day Serendipity workshop led by Lyman Coleman lit a fire for community in me, and that fire burns to this day. The idea of convening people in small groups as an *inherently valuable* activity had never really occurred to me before that workshop. The idea that church was essentially community, and the idea that average people could lead the church if it was organized in smaller pockets—these are big ideas that continue to inspire me.

Carl George's "metachurch" language never really caught on, but his *both/and* concepts certainly did, at least with me. Over the years, I have accumulated a lot of tools in my ministry toolbox, but the ones that George gave me fit my hand the best and have allowed me to accomplish the most. George saw value in both small and large gatherings of the church. He lobbied for an ecosystem of different-size conventions that would meet different needs in different ways.

G. K. Chesterton was a sage who argued eloquently against materialism, relativism, and agnosticism—corrosive ideas that took over the twentieth century. He defended the common man, and common sense. He was a proponent of the family. He was an advocate of beauty. But he also had some insights into organization, and these were particularly salient. He called his theory of government *distributism*. Distributism is based on widespread ownership of property. It means self-support, self-control, and self-government. It means people producing and using their own goods, making their own laws, and being interdependent with their neighbors. Chesterton's theory of distributism transcends economics. It is the notion of independent landowners, craftsmen, and merchants with an interest in taking part in civic life, and the economic ability to do so. It may be the sanity that the church will be looking for in the next century.

As a composite, these leaders embody the impact and the intimacy that we want to see in the church today. By "we" I mean Christian leaders who are tired of one-dimensional approaches to Christianity—tired of the idea that it's all one way or the other. By "we" I mean Christian leaders who want to hear the church in stereo. By "we" I mean Christian leaders who want to hold two ideas at the same time—that the church can be personal, and that the church can be powerful.

Hybrid Church

Introduction to Both

Carl George, the church futurist, predicted nearly twenty years ago that extremely large churches would emerge in America in the twenty-first century, and that individual churches in this country would resemble either elephants or fields of mice.[1] Both elephants and mice can do damage, if in different ways.

The assessment of Tony Dale, a microchurch expert, is that the mice are multiplying: "Our read of what is going on is that millions of Christians are moving in a simple, organic direction." Dale may actually have understated this trend. The number of people convening weekly in microchurches is in the *tens* of millions. These churches go by different names—cell church, house church, organic or simple church. Their congregations include as few as three to five people and as many as thirty. Some of the microchurch movements include homeschooling networks, biblical worldview groups, spiritual discipline groups, Christian creative arts guilds, and various marketplace ministries. As a result of random telephone research, George Barna estimates that as many at 9 percent of adults in the United States have had some experience with a microchurch.[2] And a recent Pew study backs up Barna's research, indicating that 7 percent of adults have their primary worship experience in a home or a small group.[3] If there are two hundred million adults in the United States, this comes to fourteen million, of whom ten to twelve million are Christians.

This trend may not be obvious, because the groups are disunited and disorganized (the largest of the more organized groups account for fewer than three million people). But it is precisely because these groups are not being coordinated that Dale calls the organic church "a Holy Spirit movement . . . no one but Him has enough influence to bring it about."

At the other end of the scale, the large churches are becoming even larger. Congregations of ten thousand or more people are becoming more common in the United States, with Lakewood Church in Houston, Texas, approaching fifty thousand per weekend. There are over 1,500 megachurches nationwide; the typical Protestant congregation has at least two thousand people in a typical weekend. These megachurches are growing not just in number but also in size. They had an average growth rate of 50 percent over five years, and more than 20 per cent of megachurches experienced an increase of 100 percent in a five-year period. Only 10 per cent of megachurches showed stagnation or decline.[4]

This book validates both of these trends and looks to connect the two in ways that can be synergistic. When we take a more holistic view, we see that large churches can become significant hubs in the emerging diverse, organic ecosystem of the church. And when we see the bigger picture, we understand that smaller bodies are excellent at building deep, meaningful, personal relationships and can become part of a grander story that is transforming the spiritual landscape.

Both Are Church

The church for which I am the lead pastor, Christ the King Community Church (CTK), numbers tens of thousands of participants, but I feel the need to chase that statement with another. We are one church that meets in many locations—and most of our congregations are quite small.

I guess I hasten to add this because, for me, it's not all about being big. It's also about being small. In fact, I would say that CTK has become big, not by being good at being big but by being good at being small. Our vision statement calls on us "to see a prevailing, multilocation church emerge that will transform the spiritual landscape," and we pledge to "convene in thousands of small groups with Worship Centers strategically located in every community." Our vision, in miniature, is "transformation through multiplication."

Because CTK is a network of small as well as large gatherings, we get included in lists of megachurches and microchurches alike. That is, we sometimes find ourselves lumped in with other churches of great scale because of our cumulative attendance, and yet, because small groups are the basic building block of our church, we are also sometimes characterized as a cell church or a house church. But we don't fit comfortably into either category. Whereas most churches are one or the other, we are both. We are a hybrid.

I've used the word *hybrid* so often to describe the blend that is CTK that it is probably about time that I define exactly what it is that our church brings together. We are not combining just smallness with largeness but two things that are much more significant. We are fusing *intimacy* (a personal, relational, transparent church) and *impact* (a powerful, relevant, and transformative church) to create a third form, and that is what a hybrid is. If you were to listen to people talking about our church, you would hear them revealing their preference for one aspect over the other, often by discounting the other. "I feel lost in a big church" is another way of saying, "I appreciate intimacy." "I want to go somewhere where my friends will be impressed" is a way to say, "I desire a place of impact."

If you were to meet some CTK participants (we don't have "members" but "active participants"), you would hear them tell varied stories about what they appreciate about CTK. One might say, "This is the first church where I have really gotten to know people, and where people have gotten to know me. I have grown so much because of my small group." Another might say, "I enjoy the weekend worship services. I feel the presence of

God when we get together." Still another might say, "I love the fact that we are reaching out and starting new Worship Centers in new communities." The point is that people do not experience CTK as one thing or the other but as both, as a combination that is a powerful hybrid.

Sometimes a hybrid form serves a transitional function. Between epochs, for example, we often find transitional forms that reach simultaneously back into the past and forward into the future. This is likely true right now for the automotive industry as refined fossil fuels become less plentiful and alternative forms of power, such as electricity and hydrogen, become more useful. Some people would see the hybrid church in the same light, understanding it to be a way station between the corporate, programmatic church (like the combustion engine, a popular but endangered species) and the smaller house fellowships that are projected to replace it eventually.

But I personally do not view the hybrid church as a transitional form. I view it as a preferred design. It brings two things together in a synergistic way. We prefer the two together because the whole is greater than the sum of its parts. When the church combines intimacy and impact, it gives us the best of both worlds.

Both Are Valid

Today, microchurches and megachurches alike are meeting needs and growing in popularity. Churches are getting smaller and larger at the same time. Each of these approaches to church is succeeding because of its respective strengths—intimacy for the microchurch, and impact for the megachurch. As Chesterton opines, both can and should be celebrated:

> A man may say, "I like this vast cosmos, with its throng of stars and its crown of varied creatures." But if it comes to that, why should not a man say, "I like this cozy little cosmos, with its

decent number of stars and as near a provision of live stock as I wish to see?" One is as good as the other; they are both mere sentiments. It is mere sentiment to rejoice that the sun is larger than the earth; it is quite as sane a sentiment to rejoice that the sun is no larger than it is. A man chooses to have an emotion about the largeness of the world; why should he not choose to have an emotion about its smallness?[5]

In the modern world, "Bigger and better" has been the rallying cry. Yet it has proved perilous to discount the small. Christensen chronicles the fall of Seagate, a former industry leader in hard disk drives.[6] Seagate toppled because the company was building larger and faster drives for mainframe users and missed the shift to handheld devices and minicomputers that require smaller drives. According to Peters, corporate culture itself is undergoing a shift toward smallness in our interconnected global economy:

- Fewer than 1 in 10 Americans now work for a Fortune 500 company.
- The number No. 1 private employer in the United States, by body count, is no longer GM or AT&T. It's Manpower, Inc., the temporary work mega agency.
- Between 16 and 25 million of us are freelancers or independent contractors. There are now three million temps—including temp lawyers, temp engineers, temp project managers, and even temp CEOs.
- Microbusinesses, defined as companies that employ four or fewer people, are home to as many as 27 million of us.[7]

Likewise, the number of microchurches is likely to grow as political and financial pressures mount against the corporate church. But we should not imagine that large corporations have been eradicated from the face of the earth, or that they will be eradicated any time soon. The same people who are pursuing an organic lifestyle are drinking Starbucks coffee, wearing Nike tennis shoes, and flying across the country on Boeing airplanes. The fact is, we can be well served by both the organic and the organizational, by the small and the large.

Participants in megachurches are excited about their churches, which offer quality programming, specialized staffs, and generous facilities. At the same time, and with just as much enthusiasm, those who are participants in microchurches laud the personal connectedness, care, and attention they experience in smaller fellowships.

Grant Fishbook, pastor of CTK in Bellingham, Washington, offers a directional comparison between intimacy and impact. "Impact is a springboard," he says. "Intimacy is a diving board. Impact pushes you forward. Intimacy gives you a chance to plumb the depths."

The relative contributions of megachurches and microchurches remind me of the story about a man who was looking at a river and asked a local man, standing nearby, "Is this the Mississippi?" "It's part of it," the local replied. The story is relevant to Christ's church. We want to imagine that what we're looking at is "it." And it is. But it's not all of it. Christ's church is bigger and broader than a single point in space or time, and than a single point of view.

I am a proponent of relational evangelism. I understand my primary mission field to be those in my relational circle of influence. It seems to me that evangelism works well in a relational context. But I am nevertheless very happy that my father-in-law became a Christian at a Billy Graham crusade in Los Angeles. It's not all one way or another.

Unfortunately, the simultaneous growth in participation at megachurches and microchurches has been accompanied by a growing sense of distrust and animus between these two wings of the church. In early 2009 I was invited to a meeting of megachurch and microchurch leaders in Orlando, Florida. There were about fifty key leaders in attendance. Some were from the largest churches in America (those whose attendance is greater than five thousand). Others were from the smallest microchurches in America. During the two-day discussion, we talked about how big churches can support little churches, and vice versa. But the conversation was largely superficial until the very last hour, when something significant happened. One of the microchurch pastors turned to one of the megachurch pastors and asked, "What do you need from us? What do you want from the house church?" Without skipping a beat, the megachurch pastor said, "Grace. We need grace. Quit throwing stones at the megachurch. Quit launching grenades. We need grace. We love people and want to see them become followers of Christ. We just do it in a different way than you. We need grace."

Up until that point, there had been an elephant in the room. We were talking about how to work together, but we didn't much trust each other. As I think about what happened in that room between those two pastors, the word that comes to mind—maybe a synonym for grace—is *validation*. It is incumbent upon members of the body of Christ to validate other members. What that large-church pastor was saying was "I need you to validate my ministry." Small-church pastors are also longing to be validated by large-church pastors.

There's a need for us to look at what others are doing and say, "Isn't that great!" As Paul explains in 1 Corinthians 12:21, the eye cannot say to the hand, "I don't need you!" And the head cannot say to the feet, "I don't need you!" God works in different ways at different times and places—and note that it's *ways*. We waste our time trying to figure out the one "way" in which God is at work. God is the head of the body. He is at work in various ways in people's lives.

The megachurch-microchurch contrasts are not theological or spiritual. They are philosophical and methodological. As near as I can tell, the people who participate in megachurches and microchurches love Jesus. They want His kingdom to come and His will to be done on earth, and they feel called to what they are doing. As near as I can tell, they are all interested in carrying out the great commission (though they may emphasize different aspects of it).

Both Are Effective

Both the megachurch and the microchurch can be effective. Of course, both can be ineffective as well, but I'm going to stick with the positive here—the megachurch and the microchurch done well.

A healthy, vibrant megachurch can have a great impact on you as a participant. I still remember vividly the message that Bill Hybels preached at a service I attended at Willow Creek Community Church. The video, the drama, the lighting, and the sound all came together to drive home Bill's message about reaching out to the prodigals among us. But I also remember being in a home group one night when a couple opened up about their marriage and how they were struggling. Our group literally surrounded that couple that night and interceded for them.

Military commanders are trained to look for force multipliers on the battlefield, circumstances that can give an army a two-, three-, or even fourfold advantage. Such things as weather or morale can be force multipliers. (In fact, before D-day, General Dwight D. Eisenhower spent much of his time coordinating with meteorologists to get a read on the weather.) If two armies are equivalent but one has the wind at its back, which one has the better chance of succeeding? If two armies are equivalent but one is well rested and well fed, which one would you choose? Force multipliers allow an army to "tilt" the battlefield—instead of struggling harder to climb uphill, the troops roll downhill.

Microchurches and megachurches harness different winds as force multipliers. Force multipliers for the microchurch include these factors:

1. *Prayer.* When you have a chance to share who you really are and what is going on with you, the prayers of others become much more powerful. In the CTK story, we have experienced the power of thousands of groups gathering every week and interceding for the work that needs to be done. Prayer moves the hand of God, and when God is with you, miraculous things come from ordinary inputs.

2. *Christ-centeredness.* Jesus himself tipped us off to a force multiplier: "If I be lifted up, I will draw all men to me." Lift up Christ. Worship him. Teach him. Enjoy him. When Christ is made the honored guest, when people get their eyes on Jesus and off other things, the results are renewal, life change, and spiritual refreshment.

3. *Comfortableness.* G. K. Chesterton said, "Angels can fly because they take themselves lightly."[8] Are you taking yourself and your ministry too seriously? If so, lighten up. Smile. Relax. Enjoy. As in sports, everything seems easier when you are loose. Laughter is characteristic of healthy families, and of healthy house churches.

And here are some of the force multipliers for megachurches:

1. *Faith.* Is the glass half full or half empty? Many megachurches are led by extraordinary visionaries who see the glass as half full. They are trusting God that large numbers of people will be swept into the kingdom of heaven. Their enthusiasm is infectious.

2. *Momentum.* Success begets success. When something goes well, and you celebrate that, you tend to encourage more of the same. Why is it that some teams tend to win season after season, and others tend to lose? They're practiced in victory. Once you get used to winning, you start planning on it and preparing for it. Many successful megachurches have created a positive momentum that continues to propel them into the future.

3. *Creativity*. The creativity of the megachurch is astounding. Staging, video, lighting, sound effects—it all goes to break up the monotony and make church a place where people want to go.

Both Are Imperfect

The proponents of one model of ministry or the other may trumpet its benefits, but neither the megachurch nor the microchurch is without flaws. Navigating between these flaws calls to mind Odysseus moving through the narrow passage between Scylla and Charybdis in Homer's *The Odyssey*: there is a sea monster on one side and a deadly whirlpool on the other.

When it comes to models of ministry, on one side is the danger of becoming a club. Small churches possess an ability to foster close friendships, but there are fewer people and resources with which to work. It is also sometimes difficult for the smaller assembly to muster a quality presentation from a shallow talent pool. Moreover, a small assembly can easily become insulated and ingrown, its agenda susceptible to being hijacked by the loudest voice in the group. In addition, a ministry that does not engage in making more disciples of Jesus Christ becomes inwardly focused and comes to resemble a club more than church. There are many churches of this kind—75 percent of the churches in America did not see a single convert come to Christ last year. Admittedly, there are other problems to work on, but Christ's instructions to go into the world and make disciples should not be overlooked.

On the other side is the danger of becoming a crowd. Megachurches attract crowds of people and sizable resources, but the people are often passive spectators instead of active participants. As the work of those "onstage" takes on greater importance, it becomes easier to get lost in the crowd. When a ministry becomes effective in reaching out to lost people but does not maintain an authentic Christian core, it can become

a crowd instead of a church. Community is what makes the
difference between a crowd and a church. If you get a bunch of
people in a room and there is no connection between them, it's
a crowd. If you get a bunch of people in a room and there is
relationship, it's a church.

The lesson here is that it's possible to be effective in reaching out to large numbers of unchurched people, but without a sufficient Christian community into which they can be
assimilated, it's just a greater concentration of darkness rather
than an act of drawing people out of darkness and into the
light. Evangelism and discipleship must work together in
partnership.

Both Are Misunderstood

Large churches often view small churches as anemic runts. But
that's not necessarily what they are. Bliese describes the small
congregation as carrying out a unique mission: "The myth of
size assumes that small churches are de facto struggling, paro-
chial, maintenance-oriented, at risk, and not able to compete in
today's church marketplace. . . . Breaking the myth of size means
realizing that small churches are not necessarily premature, ille-
gitimate, malnourished or incomplete versions of 'real' churches.
Small congregations are the right size to be all that God calls a
church to be."[9] It's also true that small churches are thought to be
better than they really are at some tasks, such as discipleship. But
the dirty little secret of the microchurch is that house church participants are not particularly organized. Tony Dale says that house
church participants do not utilize their resources nearly as strategically as their megachurch counterparts.

But myths about the megachurch also abound. Thumma
and Travis debunk several such myths, including the myths that
megachurches are driven by personality cults, water down the
faith, and grow because of the "worship show."[10] And Carlos
Whittaker, director of service programming at Buckhead

Church, one of the North Point Community Church campuses in the Atlanta area, blogged as follows in response to myths he has encountered as a megachurch staff member:

Myth: You can't find real relationships in a mega-church
Truth: You were not in my living room Sunday night with Heather, Zach, Meghan, and I.

Myth: Mega-Churches are a mile wide and an inch deep.
Truth: I dive deeper into the core of who this church is every week and have yet to even see the bottom. When you figure out how to love your neighbor then maybe we will dive into the hermeneutical Hebrew apostolic translations.

Myth: Mega-Churches have it all figured out.
Truth: They hired me. If this was true. It no longer is.

Myth: Because they pay musicians to play on Sunday morning, there is not as much "heart" on stage.
Truth: A paycheck does not forfeit love for God. Honestly, you not only have musicians that "have heart" on stage, you now have musicians that can play their instruments well.

Myth: Mega-Churches are built on a man. The main communicator.
Truth: I have not heard one baptism video on Sunday morning with the line "I accepted Andy Stanley into my heart and am telling the world I am living the rest of my life for him!"

Myth: Mega-Church staffs are corporate, non-relational, and stiff.
Truth: Ummmmmmmmmmmmm

Myth: Mega-Churches are too uptight with their money and should just give it all away.
Truth: Please find me the verse that says churches are supposed to be stupid with their money. I am more grateful than ever to have the financial teams we have at NPMI.

Myth: Mega-Churches should spend their money rescuing orphans with all their dollars instead of building fancy buildings.

Truth: They should rescue orphans. They should also rescue Bob the 38 year old banker who lives off of Tower Place Drive in Buckhead.

Myth: 70% of all male staff try to look like Rob Bell.
Truth: OK. You got us. This one is true.[11]

Megachurches are typically thought to be quite evangelistic, with large numbers of converts each year. But that's not necessarily so, either. The dirty little secret of the megachurch (although it's not really such a secret) is that the vast majority of their growth comes from Christians transferring from other local churches in their areas. Extensive research by Schwarz found that "the evangelistic effectiveness of mini-churches is statistically 1600 percent greater than that of the mega-churches" and that large size is one of the most negative factors in relation to church growth, if by "growth" we mean conversion growth.[12]

Both Are Biblical

The Church Growth Movement has come to associate bigger churches with better churches. Chesterton notes this fallacy that attends size: "There is unfortunately one fallacy here into which it is very easy for me to fall, even those who are most intelligent and perhaps especially those who are most imaginative. It is the fallacy of supposing that because an idea is greater in the sense of larger, that it is greater in the sense of more fundamental and fixed and certain."[13]

Throughout scripture, you see God at work in ways both big and small, with both intimacy and impact. He parts the sea, and He fills the water pot. The God who thunders also speaks in whispers. He wins with armies of hundreds of thousands, or an army of one. The Bible often celebrates small things: little David, not the giant Goliath; Gideon's small band, not the enemy hordes; the widow's mite, not the Pharisee's largesse; the cup of cold water in His name, not the grandstand play.

In God's economy, there is beauty in both the large and the small. He inhabits the tiny seed as well as the towering redwood. God works with the small and the big. He used Samson both when he was wearing a size XXL T-shirt and later in life, when he wore a size S T-shirt. In the Bible, the biggest people often hold on to something small. As Lucado recounts, "Moses had a staff. David had a sling. Samson had a jawbone. Rahab had a string. Mary had some ointment. Aaron had a rod. Dorcas had a needle."[14]

The early church, we read, met "house to house and in the temple courts"—in both places. The first-century church resembled the architecture of the Internet, an architecture of small pieces loosely joined. It convened in smaller private spaces, but it also assembled corporately in larger public spaces. Believers were getting their needs met in smaller gatherings, but they were also making a splash in the community in large conventions.

So if the megachurch and the microchurch are both biblical, then we need to embrace them both. God's truth is often in stereo: fellowship and worship, freedom and accountability, grace and holiness, justice and mercy, evangelism and discipleship, community and outreach. Smith cites a rabbinical teaching to describe the relationship:

> A king had some empty glasses. He said: "If I pour hot water into them they will crack; if I pour ice-cold water into them they will also crack!" What did the king do? He mixed the hot and the cold water together and poured it into them and they did not crack. Even so did the Holy One, blessed be He, say: "If I create the world on the basis of the attributes of mercy alone, the world's sins will greatly multiply. If I create it on the basis of the attributes of justice alone, how could the world endure? I will therefore create it with both the attributes of mercy and justice, and may it endure!"[15]

In isolation, neither side is, as Chesterton said, "quite right enough to run the whole world."[16]

Both Are Beautiful

When people realize that I am a pastor, they routinely ask, "How big is your church?" Innocent curiosity is what leads most of them to ask. What they may not realize, however, is that size is actually a significant variable that accounts for a large number of differences among churches. George says that the differences between and among tiny, small, medium, large, and extra-large churches is akin to the differences between and among mice, cats, dogs, horses, and elephants.[17] Holmes spent a year investigating her one-fifth-acre backyard in suburban Portland, Maine, and wrote a book about her adventure of discovering the wild kingdom of ants, spiders, ladybugs, and crows.[18] God's acts are astonishing, even when set forth in miniature. At the other end of the scale, one of my favorite memories is of going "backstage" at a zoo in Hyderabad, India, and coming face to face with a Bengal tiger. Mere inches (and steel bars) separated us. This singular experience was astonishing precisely because of the magnitude of the animal. There's a "wow" factor with a tiger that you don't get with a kitten.

In nature, beauty can be found in the big and the small, and the same is true of social organizations like the church. Ultimately, it is not about numbers. It is about people. It is about fulfilling the great commission and bringing people out of darkness into God's marvelous light. In that sense, the greatest intimacy is intimacy with God, and the greatest impact is the impact of God. Intimacy with God is what turns into impact, and the impact of God is what turns into intimacy.

Larger churches are able to facilitate the mission by providing services and options to a variety of age groups and needs, by providing economies of scale, and by providing competent staff and specialists. Smaller churches are able to facilitate the mission by providing personal time and attention, and by providing responses tailored to needs. It's all good.

1

THE EXTREME WORLD

Kristyn, my wife, after talking with her sister Robyn, asked me if I had heard about the Extremely Focused Church conference in Colorado (her sister was going to it). I told her I hadn't heard about it. After some research, I realized she was talking about the Externally Focused Church conference (which I had heard about). But of the two conference names (one made up, one real), I like the sound of the Extremely Focused Church conference better, and that's saying a lot, because the idea of being externally focused resonates with me a great deal. There is something to be said for being extreme, particularly in our new world, which is filled with well curves and hybrids.

It's a Well-Curve World

The bell curve is a statistical distribution pattern showing how the majority of people in a study of a particular social phenomenon will gravitate toward the middle of a range of outcomes. For example, most people have families of moderate size, are of moderate height, and get average grades. Because there are fewer extremely large families, and fewer extremely tall or short people, and fewer people who earn A's or F's, the data pertaining to these phenomena, plotted on a chart, take the form of a bell. Figure 1.1 shows a typical bell curve.

For decades, American business and culture have been formed to meet the needs of the middle range of consumers. The mass media have also been pointed toward the center. We have loved the word *general* in business—General Mills, General Motors, General Dynamics, General Electric. Mainstream culture has been organized around the general masses.

Figure 1.1 A Typical Bell Curve

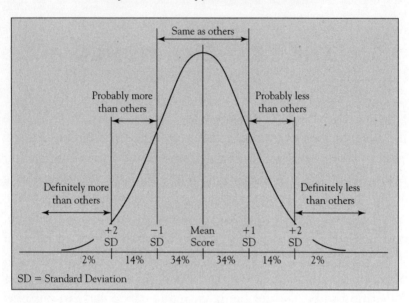

When it comes to churches, however, mainline denominations do not command the position they used to. Over the past decade, a bimodal pattern has been emerging as sociological gravitations have moved toward the ends of a surveyed range and away from the middle. Pink has used the term *well curve* to describe this new trend: "Although bell curve distribution is still considered normal, a surprising number of economic and social phenomena now seem to follow a different arc. Instead of being high in the center and low on the sides, this new distribution is low in the center and high on the sides. Call it the well curve" (see Figure 1.2).[1]

The well curve describes a world that is getting bigger and smaller at the same time. And the middle is falling out (for example, the middle class and middle management), and the extremes are becoming even more extreme (the lower and upper classes). Homes, television sets, and media are all getting larger and smaller at the same time. Bell-shaped curves are giving way to well-shaped curves, where the middle is not the high point but rather the low point. The extremes are the

Figure 1.2 The Well Curve

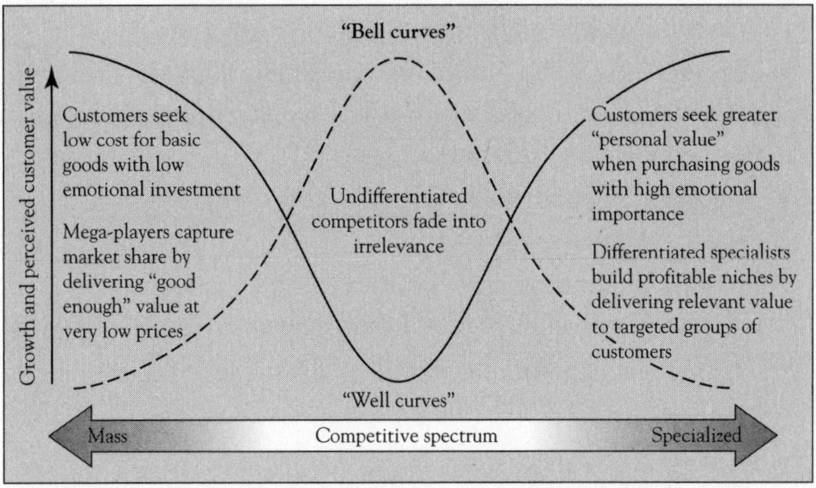

Source: IBM Institute for Business Value. The "well curver" concept was described in the following article: Pink, Daniel H. "The Shape of Things to Come," Wired. May 2003.

high points. The middle is a tar pit. Examples of the shrinking middle abound:

- The rise in sales of either very big TVs (60-inch plasma) or very small ones (incorporated into cell phones), and the severe decline in the sale of midsize ones (such as the old 27-inch TV)
- The release of more automobiles of the extremely small and big varieties, and the decline in popularity of midsize vehicles
- The growth of organizations through mergers and acquisitions, or their shrinkage through spinoffs
- The rise in huge multinational federations (NAFTA, the European Union, and so on), with the simultaneous multiplication of independent states and secessionist movements
- Increasing or shrinking portions at restaurants
- The rise in the number of students scoring in the highest and lowest ranges on standardized tests, and the drop in the number of students scoring in the middle ranges

- The increase in the number of people earning at the top and the bottom of the income scale, and the decrease in the number of people earning a middle-class income
- The increase in the number of consumers flocking either toward high-end products or toward cheap products while fleeing products in the middle ground
- The rising popularity of extreme sports—and of golf
- Increasing polarization of politics toward the left and the right, with movement away from the center
- The proliferation of megaretailers as well as of niche boutiques

The middle may still be where most people are, but it is no longer the place where most people desire to be or plan to stay. Words like *average*, *medium*, and *middle* have fallen in popularity. And whereas companies used to gravitate to the word *general*, they no longer do. The slogan for today's culture is "Wherever you end up, don't end up in the middle."

As a basketball official, I can tell you that the worst place from which to see the play is the middle of the floor, right under the basket. You are much better off at one side or the other, in order to get a wide-angle view of the court. In fact, officials are taught to imagine the area below the basket as quicksand. You don't want to find yourself there, and if you do, you want to get out of there as quickly as possible and go wide.

Even popular music has shifted away from the comfortable middle to a more dynamic range. When I was young, I was coached in how to set the equalizer on my stereo. My equalizer had sliders from low to high frequency. For best effect, I was encouraged to create a bell-shaped curve with these sliders, with lower settings of highs and lows and a greater midrange. This would not tune to the modern ear, however. Old-school pop has given way to modern jazz stylings, with a lower midrange, higher highs, and lower lows (see Figures 1.3 and 1.4).

Figure 1.3 Pop Settings for a Stereo's Equalizer

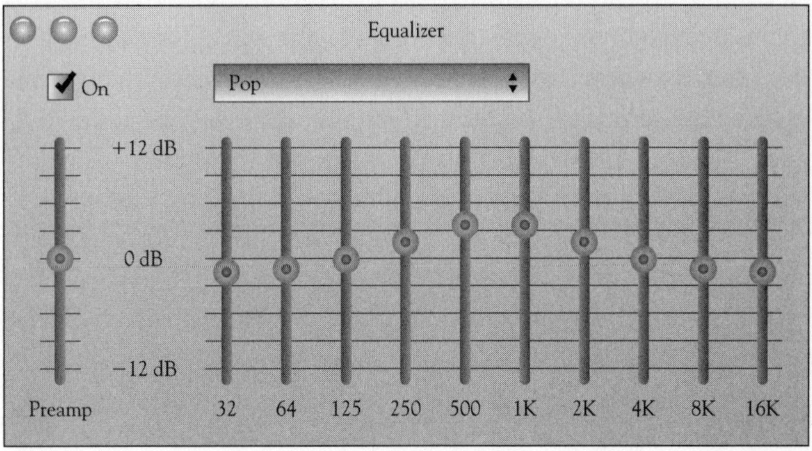

Figure 1.4 Jazz Settings for a Stereo's Equalizer

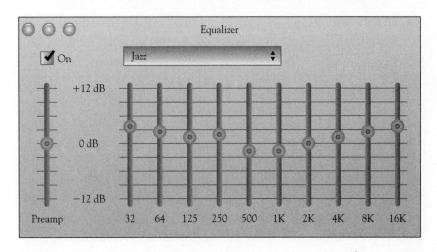

Where is the worst place to be assigned a seat on an airplane? The dreaded middle seat. What is the worst kind of drink you can be served? The room-temperature, lukewarm, "spew you out of my mouth" kind. It is much better to be either inside or outside, hot or cold.

Today the middles are in trouble, and the edges seem vital. According to Sweet, who explores this model in the realm of a chain of coffeehouses, one of the keys to the success of Starbucks is the company's gravitation toward giving the consumer an extreme experience—extreme comfort, extreme tastiness, extreme hotness.[2] Maxwell House, by contrast, is stuck in the middle. The days of the happy medium (and of a related word, *mediocre*) are gone.

How does the well curve apply to the church? Relationships are one of the areas where I don't think you can go partway and be successful. If you are going to make your ministry about relationships, then really make your ministry about relationships. Don't go halfway. You can't "kind of" make community a priority. You have to go full-on.

And how does the model of the disappearing middle apply to the church? Here are three of the many ways, according to Hall:

- *Membership.* Some congregations are raising the bar and giving membership greater emphasis; others are dropping membership.
- *Money.* There are fewer "average" givers.
- *Manpower.* There is a shrinking role for moderately involved volunteers.[3]

But I think the greatest application of this model to the church is in overall positioning. The medium-size church of a few hundred people, once prized, now doesn't seem attractive. It is neither big enough for impact nor small enough for intimacy.

And yet the brighter the light, the darker the shadows. I was talking with a friend who is a leader in a traditional denominational church. He was telling me about a worship director his church was about to hire. Evidently she is very gifted and qualified. A very proficient pianist. A very powerful vocalist. Sounded pretty good on the surface. Maybe too good, actually. The number of times my friend used the word *very* to describe her raised a red flag for me. I said to him, "Challenges often attend the word *very*." To be specific, a few years ago I hired a young lady to be a worship director. She was an extremely gifted violinist. In fact, she was so good that she is now living in Nashville, working with some of the biggest names in the music industry. She brought tremendous value onstage, but to make her compensation make sense, I also had her doing some things for me in the office (setting up small groups, answering phones, and so on). She was a way better performer than a clerk. If we could have opened up her skull, we would have found that the right side of her brain (the creative side) was musclebound and that the left side (the analytical side) was shrimpy. Corresponding to the overdeveloped part was an underdeveloped part. I call this phenomenon of the shadows that attend extremes the *bright-light quandary*. Taking the example of talent, you can see that as the light gets brighter, the shadows become more intense. What to do about the shadows? Do not turn down the light. Instead, turn on the backlight. Counterbalance with the opposite extreme. You do have to cover the blind spots, and they tend to be more dramatic the more you have to use the word *very* to describe the strength.

It's a Hybrid World

Hybrid is a hot word in our mash-up culture. Hybrid forms provide us with elements of two desired outcomes. A hybrid is an attempt to get the best of both worlds. Hybrid vehicles, for example, give us economy with performance.

There are hybrid dogs, toaster ovens, and schools. Hybrid forms result when two elements of different entities are mixed for a particular purpose. They bring together the best of two worlds. Here are some examples of hybrid forms:

In mythology, a creature combining body parts of two or
more species

In biology, the offspring resulting from cross-breeding of different plants or animals

In etymology, a word with mixed origins

In the world of bicycles, a model combining the design features of a road bike and a mountain bike

In automotive transportation, a car that combines an internal combustion engine with an electric motor

In finance, an economic vehicle that combines elements of debt and equity

In golf, a type of club that combines elements of a driver and an iron

In video games, human avatars with alien characteristics

In the world of churches, a congregation that achieves the best of both intimacy and impact

In our hybrid world, the extremes are becoming more extreme, but the poles of the emerging well curve are also being bridged in various ways.

For example, both quality and convenience are having their day in transportation. Harley-Davidson can ship four hundred thousand motorcycles per year. Confederate Motorcycle, based in New Orleans, builds high-performance $62,000 bikes but sells fewer than one hundred per year. Confederate is not trying to compete with Harley for market share. Confederate is focused on breakthrough performance and design innovations, and that's all.

You can also see combinations of higher convenience and higher quality in some business models that have come forward in the music industry. There is a place for both kinds of value. Musicians are allowing their music to be downloaded at low quality and cost (in some cases letting the consumer name the price) and at the same time they are providing high-quality concerts and CDs with extra content. In response to extremes in convenience, you are also seeing extraordinary value-added packaging. From the same artist you can now download a twelve-second ringtone of a popular song or order a four-DVD set with live concert and studio footage.

Bounty, the manufacturer of paper towels, has found that people are actually polarized over which value proposition—smallness or bigness—they favor overall. Bounty researched the reaction of people to a smaller size of paper towel (six inches by eleven inches) and found that one in four people will select a smaller towel when given the option. The company also found that many people did not want a smaller sheet at all, ever, and that they preferred the full-size square towel. Bounty's solution? The company created a paper towel from which the consumer can tear off one, two, or three sections, according to his or her needs and tastes. Do people want a smaller or a bigger towel? Yes. At different times? Yes. In different combinations? Yes.

Speaking of technology and packaging, one day I was browsing YouTube videos on my phone and caught myself avoiding the longer video clips. I did not want to have to put up with the buffering times for clips of a minute or more, and so I began to gravitate to clips that were sixty seconds or less. When I realized what I was doing, an idea came to my mind—the sixty-second sermon. The idea is pretty simple, really—a video that would include a reading of scripture, an explanation, an illustration, and a summary. In the middle of the workday, maybe at a stoplight or during a work break, a person could watch a brief sermon and have a moment of inspiration. Who says that spiritual content has to be delivered in thirty to thirty-five minutes? And yet I have sensed a growing desire for deeper Bible teaching that cannot be accommodated on a typical Sunday morning, and so I am strategizing about providing several hours of biblical and theological instruction on a weeknight.

There is demand for both. For example, as things now come at us in miniature, Johnson sees a "snacklash" in our culture, with people wanting not just want bite-size content but also the full-meal deal:

If we're truly living in a snack culture, how come so many forms of entertainment—TV shows, games, movies—are getting longer? Most of us, I suspect, have had this experience lately: You tell a friend that they simply have to start watching one of the new long-format dramas, like *Heroes* or *The Wire*. There's no question of picking it up midseason. They've got to go back and start at the very beginning—using iTunes or BitTorrent or Netflix to catch up—or they'll be utterly confused. Invariably, your sales pitch also comes with the disclaimer that they'll have to watch four or five episodes before they really get hooked. Some of the most complex shows—like *Deadwood* or *Lost*—take multiple episodes just to introduce all the main characters.

Think about that: At roughly 45 minutes an episode, that means viewers will readily invest two to three hours in a show just to get oriented. The story itself can stretch on for dozens of hours. (*The Sopranos*, for instance, should top out at nearly 75 hours when it ends this spring.) Television has always had serial narratives, but aside from soap operas, each episode was traditionally designed to stand on its own. A midseason hour of *Kojak* made perfect sense in isolation. But you'd need *Cliffs Notes* to follow a midseason installment of *24* cold.[4]

In today's culture, there is interplay across the spectrum. Just as customers want both low cost and high quality, both the personal and the professional, both the informal and the formal, both freedom and structure, both caring and competing, those of us in the church want the intimacy of smallness and the impact of bigness, if we can have both. Intimacy and impact seem to pull away from each other, like the two poles of a magnet. But they are both desirable in the church. How do we achieve a balance between the church as a close-knit family and the church as a world-changing army? We can achieve that balance in one of two ways; by heading toward the middle or by counterbalancing on the edges, just as you can balance a teeter-totter by coming to the middle and straddling the fulcrum, or by having equivalent weight applied to each end of the board. Of the two approaches, I prefer balancing by extremes, that is, becoming extreme in both respects, intimacy and impact.

In fact, extremes in two directions are actually characteristic of Christianity. As Chesterton notes, "We want not an amalgam or compromise, but both things at the top of their energy; love and wrath both burning."[5] In the area of worship, for example, if the extremes are "rockin' out" at one end of the teeter-totter and old-time hymns at the other, then it might be better for us to use an extreme version of each style in a single service—really rockin' out, and really singing hymns—than to try to put the two styles in a blender and come out with something that doesn't give us the taste of either. I know from experience that "blended" worship is not very tasty. You have to go to extremes.

In the digital world, we now have delivery mechanisms for more of everything (shorter and longer, smaller and bigger, lo-fi and hi-fi, and so on). While brief, grainy YouTube clips circulate virally online, the average length of a major motion picture has expanded from ninety minutes to over two hours. Consumers have gotten used to making choices that alternate between high fidelity and low convenience, and between low fidelity and high convenience. For instance, there are various ways in which a person can watch a movie, and there are trade-offs involved with each (see Table 1.1).

Given options across this spectrum, consumers are saying, "Yes, yes, and yes." You can watch a sitcom or a "bitcom." You can read a self-published e-book online or buy a novel in print

Table 1.1 Fidelity and Convenience

	Theatre	Home Theatre	Mobile
Fidelity	***	**	*
	Wide screens	Big-screen TV	Tiny screen
Convenience	*	**	***
	Travel, cost	Ability to pause	In pocket

at a forty-thousand-square-foot Barnes and Noble bookstore. Movies, television shows, songs, and games come packaged like cookies or chips or in large combo packs. Sporting events get encapsulated in highlight clips on ESPN but are also available on demand via satellite. Young people consume 140-word tweets while devouring six-hundred-page tomes like *Twilight* and the books in the *Harry Potter* series. There are still blockbusters in film, literature, and music, but now, because of online retailers, we are not beholden to "the man."

There is a growing appetite for cell cinema—short-subject films designed to be viewed on a palm-size screen. For example, director Frank Chindamo's Fun Little Movies studio provides original content for Sprint cell phone customers. Slowly he is luring big-screen stars like Sharon Stone to the super-small screen. Hooray for Cellywood! "Blogs reduced the newspaper to the post. In TV, it'll go from the network to the show," says Jeff Jarvis, founder of *Entertainment Weekly*.[6] As viewing habits become more atomized, people no longer watch entire shows, just the parts they care about.

The evolution from mainframe computers to the networked PC was one of the most significant cultural changes to happen in our lifetime. It forecast the shift from the centralized, top-down way of doing business to the interconnected, bottom-up way. The small can act big. The big can act small. The growth in possibilities has followed the arc of architectural innovations that shrank the size of hard disk drives from fourteen inches in diameter to eight inches, five and one-quarter inches, three and one-half inches, two and one-half inches, and now one and one-eighth inch.

Through each epoch of globalization, extremes have become empowered. But the old bell curve values greater size and performance. The new well curve presses the extreme in both directions—the bigger is getting bigger, and the smaller is getting smaller. The energy is now going in two directions, not just one. The left side of the graph, not just the right side, has been increasingly empowered (see Figure 1.5).

Figure 1.5 Direction of Energy

Bell Curve	Well Curve
→	← →
XS, S, M, L, XL	XS, S, M, L, XL
Direction of Energy	Direction of Energy

As Thomas Friedman says, the world has become smaller as it has become bigger: "In Globalization 1.0, which began around 1492, the world went from size large to size medium. In Globalization 2.0, the era that introduced us to multinational companies, it went from size medium to size small. And then around 2000 came Globalization 3.0, in which the world went from being small to tiny."[7] Meanwhile, as the world has become smaller, in the past decade large companies have grown even larger, particularly those in a position to support the newfound power of individuals to collaborate. The modern world has gone from big to small. Next stop: both. We are becoming an hourglass society, where we must learn to kiss and punch at the same time.

Sweet describes emerging combinations:

One example of how to bring the ends together in a well-curve world, and the benefits of a simultaneous engagement of both ends of the continuum, is the competing food habits of indulgence and wellness. "Contradictory consumers" are going in opposite directions at the same time. We go from Ben & Jerry's Ice Cream or Krispy Kreme Donuts to the organic salad bar or raw juice bar.

We live in a Godiva culture of indulgence layered upon indulgence lathered with a whipped-cream topping of guilty pleasures and a final red cherry of repentance. This is also a culture obsessed with weight and health consciousness. We have the highest obesity rates in the world, and eating disorders run rampant. How do you bring these "dueling extremes" of death-by-chocolates and squeaky-clean foods together?

The blended, cut-to-the-middle solution of the bell-curve world was to introduce low-cal, low-fat chocolate. That didn't work. Why eat chocolate if you can't enjoy the fat-drenched flavor of decadence? People want the experience of luxurious chocolate. They don't want halfway, diluted experiences of chocolate. But they also want a responsible weight-management program, one that can make a difference and not just create delusions of health.

The key is to offer consumers two opposite experiences at the same time. Hence portion-controlled chocolates. Nestle's Butterfinger Stixx and Hershey's Sticks offer the binge experience of chocolate in a way that doesn't adversely impact the body. Hershey's Sticks, with a tagline promising a "convenient guilt-free way to indulge in chocolate," is available in an eleven-gram, sixty-calorie bar, with a choice of milk, dark, caramel, or mint-flavored chocolate. In a similar vein, Nabisco has introduced 100 Calorie Packs (portion-control versions of indulgent snacks such as Oreos and Cheese Nips).[8]

Part of CTK's appeal is that you will often find us at both ends of the teeter-totter. Instead of being a church that is somewhere in between big and small, or neither big nor small, we've become extremely big as a network and quite small as individual groups and centers. We've expanded rapidly by simultaneously strengthening the core and expanding the frontier. We've been engaging because our services present bleeding-edge music with old-fashioned biblical teaching. We've reached a balance by being extremely graceful and truthful, not by being slightly both. There is a danger today of getting caught in the quicksand of the middle ground. Go to extremes.

2

THE FALLACY OF EITHER/OR

I grew up in a small fundamentalist church. It was a church where everyone knew everyone else, and where visitors were easily spotted. It was a church where the phrase "It takes a village to raise a child" played out beautifully. The pastor knew everyone's name, the board of deacons rarely changed, and the Christian school kept us connected all week long.

Looking back, I see that there was something very beautiful about that experience. But because it was all intimacy and little impact, it gave me a pretty big push on a roller-coaster-like search for perspective on the merits of intimacy and impact, and on which of the two is preferable. My journey went through seven stages:

1. *Big is wrong, small is right.* This is was what I thought when I was a kid. I was pretty certain that if it was big, it must not be biblical. "They must be watering it down," I reasoned, in circular fashion, "because if they were preaching the truth, the way we are preaching the truth, then they would be small, like us." I was steeped in a small-church mentality: we did not want to get big, and because we did not want to get big, big must be wrong, because we would obviously want it if it were right. Right?

2. *Big is amazing, small is a bore.* Okay, I admit that this was a big shift for me, but I made it. The transition happened when a lot of radical changes tend to happen—when I was a teenager. Sometime when I was about fifteen or sixteen years old, I looked around and realized that I was one of only a

few teenagers in our little church. Small didn't seem so cool anymore. Jesus said "Where two or three are gathered, I am there," but that doesn't mean he doesn't like a bigger crowd. All of a sudden my small church seemed a little too small because there was no one with whom I could experience fellowship. I looked across the fence, and the grass seemed greener. On the other side I saw big churches—megachurches—that were having a mega-impact with their large youth programs and youth centers. My first exposure to the megachurch left me with my jaw dropped. This was a church that didn't have hundreds of people attending each week, but thousands. It had the biggest choir I had ever seen. It brought people in on buses from around the city. People were accepting Jesus and becoming baptized. What really damaged my previous skepticism was that they were preaching the Gospel, even throwing in some occasional fire and brimstone, but they were drawing a crowd. When I finally saw a church making an impact, I was so drawn to it that I swung from one extreme to the other and have been searching for homeostasis ever since.

3. *Big is the goal, small is a waste of time.* As I made my way into young adulthood and attended Bible college and seminary, I intensified my newfound fascination with all things grand and glorious. I decided that there was really no point in pastoring unless I was going to do it in a big way, with a big church. As a twenty-two-year-old youth pastor in a dying denominational church, I chafed under the shortsightedness of the leadership. As a young senior pastor (too young, really—I was twenty-four), I got my hands on every book I could find about church growth. I attended every seminar I could find. I made my pilgrimage to Willow Creek. I enrolled in a doctoral program at Overlake Christian Church, the largest church in the Northwest at the time. I started to work the angles to grow my church. My church did indeed grow, but I didn't, and I left that church—and the ministry, for that matter—fairly disillusioned. The church had

never been bigger. I had never been smaller. My pursuit of big was about me, not about Him.

4. *Big is easy, small is hard.* When I returned to church—as a humbled soul in the back row of Christ the King Church in Laurel, Washington—CTK was clustering on two campuses and at five services. The vibe was cool and chaotic, but meeting in two different places was obviously hard on the staff. Shortly after I joined the staff, we consolidated everything and everybody into a larger building. This wasn't my idea, necessarily, but I had to admit that the consolidation made things easier and more efficient.

5. *Big is bad, small is better.* When I struck out on my own and started CTK in Mount Vernon, Washington, I spoke highly of meeting in smaller congregations. I told the story of CTK meeting at multiple locations and in multiple services. I said, "We're not going to ask everyone to come to us, we are going to ask us to go to them." I had come to the conclusion that *more* was better than *bigger*. In an effort to make my case, I probably overstated the badness of bigness. I was questioning bigness as the accepted measure of success. I started asking questions like "Isn't the goal reaching a community instead of building a church?" At times, when it seemed like no one was listening, I turned up the volume and then backed that up with some action. As CTK in Mount Vernon grew, we "spun off" groups of people in six neighboring towns. But at the same time, Mount Vernon continued to grow bigger as well, and to this day it is our biggest Worship Center.

6. *Big is big, small is small, and both are both good and bad.* Lately, I've come to a more tempered view of bigness. I don't think bigness is as great as some people have made it out to be, but I don't think bigness is as bad as some people make it out to be, either. I don't think small is as wonderful as some people do, but I also don't see it as a problem. Big is simply big, and small is merely small. They both have corresponding trade-offs.

7. *Big is what we want, small is what we want.* When I started out on this journey, I did not have the maturity to know that it's both/and, not either/or. I felt I had to make a decision about which side of the fence I wanted to be on. I jumped the fence, only to crawl back across, and now I find myself tearing the fence down. Ancient church leaders warned of the church behaving like a drunken peasant, climbing on his donkey from one side, only to fall off the other. Jim Collins, author of *Good to Great*, labels this either/or thinking "the Tyranny of the Or":

> Having one side of this dichotomy going without the other doesn't work. In a number of professions, such as law and medicine, in academia, and in industries such as health care and the utilities, people have traditionally had a very strong core ideology, a strong sense of what they are doing. But they didn't do the other side well, the side of stimulation, progress, and change. Then people began to see that the world is changing. "We have got to be more efficient and effective," they said. "We have got to think about things like markets and segmentation and costs and cycle times." And that's all true.
>
> But they get caught up in what we call "the Tyranny of the Or," the belief that you cannot live with two seemingly contradictory ideas at the same time, that you can have change or stability, you can be conservative or bold, you can have low costs or high quality—but never both. Our visionary companies all operate in what we call "the Genius of the And," the ferocious insistence that they can and must have both at once.
>
> One "Tyranny of the Or" in health care is the assumption that becoming more businesslike means giving up the social purpose of health care. Ironically, it might benefit people in health care to study these for-profit corporations that have strong ideologies, many of them even somewhat altruistic—to see that they don't have to give up the roots of what they are about,

their reason for existence, in order to change, to become more efficient and businesslike.[1]

"The Tyranny of the Or" emanates from a misunderstanding of happiness. We tend to think that if we had more of one thing in our lives, we would be happier. For instance, if we made more money, we'd be truly happy. So we pursue that goal relentlessly, only to find out that in our obsession to make more money we have neglected our families. This sort of goal obsession is tragically commonplace.

In the movie *The Bridge on the River Kwai*, British prisoners of war in Burma are building a bridge for their Japanese captors. But it's not just any bridge. It's a beautiful one. At the end of the film there is a challenging moment when another group of Allied commandos forces the captives to consider blowing the bridge up to keep Japanese trains from using it. It becomes a very difficult decision because of the extraordinary effort that has gone into building the bridge. The men have become so focused on the beauty of their bridge that they have forgotten their larger mission of winning the war.

The church is not immune to the allure of being one thing or the other. But what if the church is meant to be both? Lyle Schaller, a church expert, was asked, "Will the church that thrives in the postmodern era be larger or smaller?" "Yes," Schaller replied. "The church of tomorrow will be both larger and smaller."

Both larger and smaller? Yes. In fact, I believe that when the church has thought "large," it hasn't thought large enough, and when it has thought "small," it hasn't thought small enough. What we have thought of as large has been in terms of thousands, but I believe that the church of the future will be include tens of thousands, hundreds of thousands, or millions. What we have thought of as small has been the small group of seven to ten people, but I believe that the church of the future will be built with even smaller conventions of two to three people.

The church of the future is going to look like the church of the past. The first-century church, for instance, met in cells and celebrations. It was both larger (in public settings like the temple courts) and smaller (in cozier settings like homes). These kinds of constructs are as possible in the postmodern world as they were in the premodern world. But before we can embrace "the Genius of the And," we need to dispel "the Tyranny of the Or."

I believe that for the church this is a homeostatic moment. In the natural world, the law of homeostasis says that an organism tends to stay in balance until some outside force disrupts the organism and causes it to become out of balance. Once we are out of balance we will take action, however, to come back into balance. Such is the case for spiritual organisms like the church as well. The modern world has acted on the church in such a way as to cause it to become imbalanced in the direction of method and manner, but the Spirit is wooing the church back to Master and mission.

Many Christians aspire to belong to a church that is either large or small. They may tend to validate the positive aspects of their particular preferences and discount the negatives. This filtering, commonly referred to as looking through rose-colored glasses, does not reflect a mature perspective, of course. Maturity moves you away from extreme, polarized reactions that blind you to certain aspects of truth. When we are no longer manic about the parts we like, we can see the reality of other parts of the picture. If we have enjoyed belonging to a large ministry, we will still be able to appreciate a smaller one. If we feel at home in an unstructured setting, we will still be able to appreciate the value of structure.

One of the beautiful gifts for those of us involved with the hybrid church is that we get to not only appreciate but also experience the other perspective. The hybrid church is not perfect, but it is inclusive of both sides of the spectrum, big and small. Elephants and mice have their respective strengths and their attendant weaknesses (see Table 2.1).

There are takeaways from Table 2.1. To begin with, there are pros and cons associated with each approach to church, of course, but this obvious point is often overlooked. If you are seeking a perfect expression of church—all upside, no downside—you will be disappointed. There are trade-offs, as would be expected, since organizations are just extensions of the people who comprise them, and people certainly come with strengths as well as weaknesses.

Moreover, the weaknesses of each approach correspond directly to that approach's strengths. It is precisely because a megachurch is established that change can be so slow. It is exactly because a microchurch is so mobile that it can seem flighty. To put this point another way, behind each of an approach's strengths is a shadow that becomes darker as the strength becomes greater. A two-hundred-year-old legacy church, for example, has the advantage of being well established in the community, but because it is so well established, it can take on the characteristics of a monument more than those of a vibrant, living spiritual community.

In addition, practitioners are typically promoters of their own approaches, and in their presentations they naturally tend to

Table 2.1. Elephant/Mega and Mouse/Micro Contrast

	Elephant/Mega	*Mouse/Micro*
Visibility	Noticeable/suspicious	Stealthy/hidden
Ethos	Exciting/impersonal	Personal/common
Flexibility	Established/slow	Mobile/flighty
Options	Singular/broad	Tailored/divergent
Resources	Significant/required	Inexpensive/meager

focus on the pros, conveniently overlooking the cons. Megachurch participants tend to rejoice in the fact that large churches are noticeable, exciting, established, broad, and significant, and they conveniently overlook the fact that a megachurch casts a large shadow, and that in this shadow are impersonality as well as the need for extraordinary resources just to keep the megachurch going. Likewise, microchurch participants tend to extol the beauty of a church that is personal, mobile, tailored to its members, and inexpensive to run, but they tend to ignore the fact that their groups are difficult to find and often insular when it comes to accepting new members.

The pros and cons that come with being a huge elephant of a megachurch are the reverse of those that come with being a tiny mouse of a microchurch. This fact gives rise to the pendulum swings that we see when people shift from enchantment to disenchantment with respect to one form of church or the other. People may "flip" on the megachurch—"It's so impersonal. We don't know anyone!"—and move to a house church, only to find out that the well-crafted presentations and excitement of the megachurch are missing from the informal microchurch setting. Conversely, the initial buzz that longtime microchurch members get when they switch to an established megachurch tends to fade over time as they realize that they have become small fish in a big pond.

When church participants switch one set of possibilities and problems for another, they are often guilty of what Rath calls "the rounding error," the unrealistic expectation that someone else will or should be able to meet all our needs.[2] I would suggest that it is equally unrealistic to expect all one's needs to be met by one church, or one church's approach.

No one has all the pieces of the puzzle. Unrealistic expectations are prerequisite to an unfulfilled life. If you are married, you can become deluded into thinking that your spouse needs to meet all your needs. Where you can become particularly vulnerable to seduction is by being attracted to the ways the other person makes up for what is missing in your spouse. People tend to fall in love with the possibilities but have to learn to live with the problems. When the honeymoon period is over and reality starts to set in, you realize that your spouse has warts and wrinkles that you didn't notice on your wedding day. When someone comes along who has that missing piece, you can mistakenly think you have finally found the person who meets all your needs. In actuality, you may have found someone who brings fewer pieces to the table than your spouse but just so happens to have the one piece your spouse did not. The temptation to exchange one set of problems for another is true for groups of people as well. When church participants switch one set of possibilities and problems for another, it can mirror the dynamics that accompany romantic affairs. No one church model has all the pieces of the puzzle. Megachurches and microchurches both hold important pieces of the puzzle, but they also have empty spaces where pieces should be.

The Ups and Downs of Being an Elephant

The megachurch has been likened to an elephant, and there are ups and downs that come with being an elephant or having one around. An elephant leaves big footprints, and people notice when one is present. But elephants are slow-moving and require extraordinary resources to be sustained. They are not very cuddly, so in that way they don't make good pets. If you have a circus tent to put up, however, an elephant can pull a load.

When I go to the zoo or the circus, I enjoy seeing the elephants. There is something alluring about being around one of the largest mammals on earth. Elephants are a novelty by virtue of their being extreme in regard to size. What I feel around them is not unlike the feeling I've had at megachurch conferences I have attended. Standing, as I have, in the food court of Willow Creek Community Church, or in the outdoor pavilion of Saddleback Community Church, or in the auditorium of Lakewood Church, or near the satellite dishes outside Life Church, I can only form one word: *Wow!*

And yet some of these very churches are also lightning rods for criticism and cynicism because of the not-all-good impact they have had on their surrounding environments. Some people even see megachurches as the Wal-Marts of religion. Like Wal-Mart, they exert disproportionate influence, dwarfing smaller attractions. Just as scale creates buying power that can prove helpful to the consumer but can also lead people to have a love-hate relationship with a market leader, and just as people can grow to resent perennial favorite teams (such as the Yankees, the Lakers, or the Duke Blue Devils) and decide to cheer for the underdogs, an organization can appear to be too successful so that public sentiment shifts, and the organization's success ends up being a liability instead of an asset, as Godin says has happened:

> Big used to matter. Big meant economies of scale. (You never hear about "economies of tiny" do you?) Years ago, people, usually guys, often ex-marines, wanted to be CEO of a big company. The Fortune 500 is where people went to make a fortune, after all. Big meant power and profit and growth. Big meant control over supply and control over markets.

> There was a good reason for this. Value was added in ways that suited big organizations. Value was added with efficient manufacturing, widespread distribution, and very large R&D staffs. Value came from hundreds of operators standing by and from nine-figure TV ad budgets. Value came from a huge sales force.

> Of course, it's not just big organizations that added value. Big planes were better than small ones, because they were faster and more efficient. Big buildings were better than small ones because they facilitated communications and used downtown land quite efficiently. Bigger computers could handle more simultaneous users.

Get Big Fast was the motto for start-ups, because big companies can go public and find more access to capital and use that capital to get even bigger. Big accounting firms were the place to go to get audited if you were a big company, because a big accounting firm could be trusted. Big law firms were the place to find the right lawyer, because big law firms were a one-stop shop.

And then small happened.

Enron (big) got audited by Anderson (big) and failed (big). the World Trade Center was a terrorist target. Network (big) TV advertising is collapsing so fast you can hear it. American Airlines (big) is getting creamed by JetBlue (think small). Boing Boing (four people) has a readership growing a hundred times faster than the New Yorker (hundreds of people).[3]

Big computers are silly. They use lots of power and are not nearly as efficient as properly networked Dell PCs (at least that's what they use at Yahoo! And Google). Big boom boxes are replaced by tiny iPod Shuffles. (Yeah, I know big-screen TVs are the big thing. An exception proves the rule.) In current-day culture, centralized power can seem suspicious. In this respect, the mega-church is facing into a headwind. As Frederick the Great said, "To multiply small successes is precisely to build one treasure after another. In time one becomes rich without realizing how it has come about." The elephant does not get the luxury of taking small bites. They do not sneak up on you very well.

There is no denying, though, that elephants are a fun ride. Or so I have been told. The one time that I had the opportunity to ride an elephant (at a zoo in India), the elephant became too ill to take riders (maybe he saw me coming). But it is not unusual to hear pastors of large, thriving churches talk about the ride they are on. Unfortunately, though, the thrill may fade over time. The larger the organization, the more slowly it grows. The ride slows down. Exponential growth rates are reserved for small and medium-size organizations. The law of large numbers slows the pace.

Some have prematurely placed the megachurch on the endangered species list, but large churches are not going anywhere, anytime soon. In the United States, anyway, the attractional model is still getting quite a bit of traction. People like to go where other people go. Crowds create credibility. Americans enjoy quality music, graphics, and communication. They appreciate clever programming pointed at their kids. They like one-stop shopping. Some of the best elements of the modern world are present in the corporate megachurch. There is a psychographic element emerging in the culture that has a disdain for large corporations and slick presentations, but that group has existed in parallel to the modern world all along. In the 1960s, we called the members of this group *hippies*. But these are eddies that spin off the mainstream, and they should not be confused with the mainstream itself.

Megachurches are going to be with us for the foreseeable future, but many of them are finding it a challenge to adjust to the exploding niches of society. Nevertheless, by spinning off into smaller organizations, megachurches are able to maintain the creative spirit that smaller organizations maintain more easily.

For example, the average file-trading network traffics more music than any music store. The Internet has had a profound impact on collaboration and distribution, giving rise to smaller niches, viral hits, and "long tails."[4] Over 25 percent of the revenue of Amazon.com comes from sales that are outside the top one hundred thousand titles. Music fans, given a broader palette of choices, have grown to appreciate possibilities beyond the blockbuster hit that used to draw them to the music store on release day.

Large cities are busy creating microneighborhoods—demographic zones of retail and community life, cities within the city. Large corporate mergers, very common in the 1980s and 1990s, have fallen out of favor on Wall Street. Gigantism doesn't work. Studies indicate that most corporate megamergers don't pan out. One *Business Week* study put the merger failure rate precisely at 61 percent. Other studies show the failure rate to be as high as 80 percent. David Lascelles, codirector of the Centre for the Study of Financial Innovation, sees merger as contrary to nature, particularly when it comes to bees. Lascelles asks, "What lessons can the bees teach us . . . ? A simple one: merging is not in nature. [Nature's] process is the exact opposite: one of growth, fragmentation and dispersal. . . . Bee colonies know when the moment has come to split up into smaller colonies which can grow value faster."[5] By spinning off into smaller organizations, megachurches are able to maintain the creative spirit that is easier to maintain in the smaller organization.

No longer is there a prevailing loyalty to the big brands and bands. Anderson sees popular taste as a vestige of poor supply-and-demand matching: the favorites have been the favorites because they were the only ones you could find. That is, we have not necessarily gotten what we've wanted, only what the big shops wanted us to want. As Chesterton once said, "The monopolists' shops are really very convenient—to the monopolist. They have all the advantage of concentrating business as they concentrate wealth, in fewer and fewer of the citizens."[6]

The information age has revealed that the mainstream is not as wide as we thought. For instance, through mass media advertising there are really not that many options presented to the public. The top one hundred advertisers account for more than 87 percent of all advertising expenditures in this country. The big bets of big business tend to be conservative and predictable, as illustrated in the making of major motion pictures:

> Setting out to a make a hit is not exactly the same thing as setting out to make a good movie. There are things you do and don't do in the quest to draw tens of millions of paying viewers. You do pay as much as you can for the biggest-name star you can lure to the project. You don't try to be "too smart." You do have

a happy ending. You don't kill off the star. If it's an action movie, more effects are better than fewer. And, all things being equal, it probably *should* be an action movie. Certainly, it's possible to break these rules and still have a hit, but why take chances? After all, you're investing a lot of money.

This hit-driven mindset has leaked outside of the Hollywood boardrooms and into our national culture. We have been conditioned by the economic demands of a hit machine to expect nothing less. We have internalized the bookkeeping of entertainment risk capital.[7]

Megachurch leaders can see a new world emerging, but they are often challenged to adjust to our rapidly diversifying culture, where bigness and smallness are merging. In some cases, the inertia that can attend girth makes change daunting. In other cases, fear of failure is pushing back, as Godin notes: "Too often, big companies are scared companies, and they work to minimize any variation."[8] In still other cases, the leaders of large churches find it difficult to build a cogent case for entering smaller "markets," particularly if doing so does not result in positive cash flow. And other leaders feel a need to keep doing things on a grand scale. Then there are the complexity and the lead time involved in synchronizing activities over a number of departments and levels when a change effort is under way. Regardless of the nature of the inertia, the process of bringing change to the megachurch is like waltzing with a gorilla or trying to turn a battleship. Elephants aren't going anywhere anytime soon, but sometimes you wish they could be a little more nimble and accommodating instead of waddling so slowly. Among the obstacles to growth that large churches face, McIntosh identifies poor assimilation of newcomers, increased bureaucracy, inadequate communication, loss of vision, and lack of member care.[9]

Some of the "waddling" of a megachurch comes from the bureaucracy that naturally attends a larger organization. In business, for example, as a company grows, "processes, procedures, checklists, and all the rest begin to sprout up like weeds. What was once an egalitarian environment gets replaced with a hierarchy. Chains of command appear for the first time. Reporting relationships become clear, and an executive class with special perks begins to appear. . . . The creative magic begins to wane as some of the most innovative people leave, disgusted by the burgeoning bureaucracy and hierarchy. The exciting start-up transforms into just another company, with nothing special to recommend it."[10]

Another cost of being an elephant is that is more difficult to innovate, and to do so quickly. To take another example from the business world, one study of companies in California found that the cost of innovation was twenty-four times greater in a large company, constrained by rules and regulations, than in a small one. The contrast is reminiscent of that seen in *Gulliver's Travels*, with the giant tied down and the little guys running around doing what they want to do.

Like elephants, megachurches require extraordinary resourcing. They are captive to the financial structure inherent in their value proposition. The good news, of course, is that the megachurch can amass the resources needed for its work, even though doing so may require persistent emphasis. The average megachurch income was $6.5 million in 2007, up from $4.7 million in 1999.[11] According to Symonds, in 2005 Willow Creek Community Church, in South Barrington, Illinois, was serving the twenty-one thousand people who attend its weekly services with a budget of $48 million; the church had $143 million in net assets and 427 employees.[12] By contrast, a traditional church with two hundred members might have a budget of $100,000. A house fellowship, led by volunteers and convening in someone's living room, is often without a budget at all. Some house fellowships even give 100 percent of their offerings to the needy in their communities. There is a rising tide against the notion that bigger must be better.

The Ups and Downs of Being a Mouse

Whereas "the next big thing" has traditionally been the locus of influence in our culture, the interconnected world has given rise to "the butterfly effect"—the notion that a small action can have a sweeping effect when amplified throughout a network. As Robert Musil observes in his classic novel *The Man Without Qualities*, "The social sum total of everybody's little everyday efforts, especially when added together, doubtless releases far more energy into the world than do rare heroic feats. This total even makes the single heroic feat look positively minuscule, like a grain of sand on a mountaintop with a megalomaniacal sense of its own importance."

The microchurch has been likened to a mouse, and mice also have their ups and downs. Mice are quick on their feet, eat very little, and can get into small spaces. But mice don't leave much of a mark on this world. Or maybe I should say, mice don't leave much of a *perceptible* mark on this world.

Galli writes about being surprised at his experience at an "irrelevant" church he attended, when his plans to attend a well-known megachurch fell through. He describes being greeted upon his arrival by a woman pulling weeds in front of the church sign. She became his personal escort, taking him into the sparsely populated auditorium, where he was introduced to several others. The weed puller then strapped on a guitar and, accompanied by a couple of singers and a drummer, proceeded to lead a less-than-stellar rendition of various worship songs. Communion was introduced informally, without the rigid protocol found in established traditions. Prayer requests were taken, and people spoke out their concerns for safe travels, sicknesses, and dealing with discouragement. But Galli was especially blessed during the announcement time, when the pastor gave a report on the church's efforts to stock the local food bank. As the pastor announced that the church has served more than twenty thousand people with food over the past ten years, the congregation broke into applause. Galli saw a sincerity in these people that was divine. After the service, his family was invited to dinner by several of the congregants, even though they realized that Galli and his family would not be returning. In the case of this small church, the inspiration did not come from the performance of the band or the slickness of the pastor. It came from hearts filled with sincerity and hospitality.[13]

Not everyone thinks of the small church as an absolutely necessary part of the spiritual ecosystem, but it is, just as small vegetation has a purpose in a forest. To take one example, I have a friend who for twenty years has picked mushrooms out in the woods. But one day as he was walking to his car with a plastic bag full of 'shrooms, a police officer pulled up and informed him that what he was doing was illegal. My friend was mystified that anyone would care if he picked a few mushrooms, so he went to the forest service to inquire. Sure enough, a law had been passed outlawing the removal of the fungi from the forest floor, because of their role in the ecosystem. Most of the mushrooms growing on the forest floor are intimately linked to trees by symbiosis. This association, called *mycorrhiza*, occurs between the root ends of a tree and the vegetative system of a mushroom. Mycorrhiza benefits both organisms—there is an exchange of nutrients, with one organism providing to the other what it cannot synthesize or extract from the soil by itself. In general, the mushroom helps the tree extract minerals and water from the soil; in exchange, the tree supplies the mushroom with sugar compounds (carbohydrates).

In just this way, the role of the small becomes clearer when you see it in relation to the system it serves. What initially seems insignificant actually serves a greater purpose than we might realize. To take another example, elephants have an inefficient digestive system. They leave lots of nutrition in their detritus. But the elephant's loss is the termite's gain. Termites routinely build mounds (skyscrapers, really) that are three thousand times their size, utilizing the dung that the elephants leave behind for nutrition and structure. Peters describes this dynamic:

> Let's say a termite construction site (mound-to-be) is 200 yards from an elephant watering hole, where dung is plentiful. The termites' "GPS" somehow locks on to the dung warehouse, and the creatures then proceed with a precision-guided underground assault. But they don't leave their mound empty-mouthed; each lugs a monstrously large grain or two of sand or soil. Soon our raiders pop up under the dung site and extract succulent morsels that the elephant had grabbed from a tree 25 feet above the ground. In place of the extracted food parcel, the termites deposit their grains of soil or sand.[14]

In the grand ecosystem of God's kingdom, small groups and house fellowships, like the termites, find that their presence is largely underground. But they are hard at work, meeting needs in a granular way. Over the course of the past five decades, as large churches have become even larger, a small-group movement has emerged and taken the place of the traditional Sunday school. Attendance at Sunday school has been dropping over the decades, but, according to Lyle Schaller, "the number of participants in weeknight Bible study classes, mutual support groups, recovery programs, prayer cells, and other expressions of the small-group movement have grown in the tens of millions." The microchurch has put us in touch with the fact that Christ will be present whenever two or three gather in His name.

The modular and mobile nature of the small group is one of its chief attractions. Groups can convene at any time, in any place. At CTK, we say that we can have as many groups as we have leaders and living rooms. This approach is more like guerrilla warfare than conventional warfare, although even Napoleon dispersed his troops in limitless patterns: instead of striking a single decisive blow, Napoleon planned a series of smaller blows against scattered adversaries. Likewise, during

World War II, Rommel's tank divisions kept the British off guard by moving quickly in many directions at incredible speed. They literally stirred up so much dust on so many fronts that they gave the impression of being a much larger force than was actually on the attack. In the same way, the microchurch is able to "peck away" and accumulate small gains on a number of fronts without being noticed. But it's also true that when you are tiny, you won't often be noticed unless you stir up some dust—or until the trouble you're creating accumulates in a noticeable way. One mosquito flying by will not be noticed. But when it buzzes in your ear or bites your arm, you notice. When a large group of mosquitoes swarms around you, that definitely gets your attention!

Bonabeau, Dorigo, and Theraulaz suggest that modern organizations can learn a lot from the swarms, flocks, and herds we see in nature.[15] For example, ants are simple creatures, yet they can perform complicated tasks, and these authors suggest that organizations can pick up a trick or two from the algorithms of ant colonies. Ants create highways leading to food, organize the distribution of larvae in the anthill, form cemeteries by clustering dead ants, build living bridges to cross gaps in their way, and assign tasks as needed, without any centralized control.

Smaller is an option now because it can be. I'm writing this paragraph on a laptop computer, in a coffeehouse served by a wi-fi network. This is no big deal nowadays. It cost the purveyor less than $50 for the wireless router, and he installed it himself. The power is to the people. As Godin writes, "Today, little companies often make more money than big companies. Little churches grow faster than worldwide ones. Little jets are way faster (door to door) than big ones."[16] Air travel, like nearly every industry, is being revolutionized by the empowerment of advancing technology. Extremely popular microjets, at roughly $1.5 million to $2.5 million, cost a fraction of the bigger, more luxurious corporate jets at more than $40 million, giving rise to point-to-point travel and reinvigorating smaller airports across the country.

"Micropolitan" areas have proved to be hubs in the emerging economy. Rural areas served by small towns used to be designated nonmetropolitan areas. But, as Anderson says, "The economics of blockbusters is not the only economics that works. Blockbusters are the exception, not the rule."[17] In fact, the larger an event, the rarer it is. So the government has created a new label, *micropolitan*, because micropolitan areas do more than fill the gaps between major cities. They are lucrative and untapped markets, as Wal-Mart has known for years. And these "rurban" areas have many ancillary benefits: land costs are lower, people are less transient, and competition is less rigorous.

According to Gladwell, small communities tend to be more unified and cohesive than larger groups, particularly groups of fewer than 150:

> If we want groups to serve as incubators for contagious messages, then as they did in the . . . early Methodist church, we have to keep groups below the 150 Tipping Point. Above that point, there begin to be structural impediments to the ability of the group to agree and act with one voice. If we want to, say, develop schools in disadvantaged communities that can successfully counteract the dangerous poisonous atmosphere of their surrounding neighborhoods, this tells us that we're probably better off building lots of little schools than one or two big ones. The Rule of 150 says that congregants of a rapidly expanding church, or the members of a social club, or anyone in a group activity banking on the epidemic spread of shared ideals needs to be particularly cognizant of the perils of bigness. Crossing the 150 line is a small change that can make a big difference.[18]

People tend to affiliate naturally with groups that are not so big that they cannot get to know others who belong to the group. According to researchers, this means groups of several hundred or fewer. Bill Gates, who has thrown billions into health and education, has conducted research through his foundation that indicates that small school size, while not an end in itself, is associated with higher attendance and higher graduation rates, stronger test scores, and less violence. The smaller setting lets each child count on the fact that there are adults who will know him and care about him at school. Likewise, surveys in business find that employees of small companies have much higher job satisfaction than those in larger companies, even though the employment costs at small companies run only about 55 percent of those at the blue-chip giants.

The promise of community is one of the outstanding promises of a smaller church. Godin sees the beauty in small:

> Small means that the founder is involved in a far greater percentage of customer interactions. Small means the founder is close to the decisions that matter and can make them quickly.

> Small is the new big because small gives you the flexibility to change your business model when your competition changes theirs.

> Small means you tell the truth on your blog.

> Small means that you can answer e-mail from your customers.

> Small means that you will outsource the boring, low-impact stuff like manufacturing and shipping and billing and packing to others while you keep all the power because you invent something that's remarkable and tell your story to people who want to hear it.

> A small law firm or accounting firm or ad agency is succeeding because they're good, not because they're big. So smart, small companies are happy to hire them.

> A small restaurant has an owner who greets you by name.

> A small venture fund doesn't have to fund big, bad ideas in order to put their capital to work. They can make small investments in tiny companies with good ideas.

> A small church has a minister with time to visit you in the hospital when you're sick.

It is better to be the head of Craigslist or the head of UPS?

Small is the new big only when the person running the small thinks big.

Don't wait. Get small. Think big.[19]

Ironically, however, the small group's promise of intimacy is a promise that frequently goes unfulfilled. Smaller communities can sometimes be more insular toward outsiders than larger ones, where relationships are more dynamic and fluid. When existing relationships are deep and long-standing, the newcomer is faced with a much more strenuous vetting process until he or she is at last accepted by the group and feels at home.

Microchurches promise less bureaucracy than larger churches. Creativity and flexibility also tend to go up in a smaller group, and smaller groups tend to be more adaptive to changing environments, whereas a larger group requires some kind of hierarchical structure or management system in order to avoid the chaos that can result from failed communication.

Here again, though, the microchurch's promise of freedom must be protected. Many people will tell you that they have found small churches that have as many barriers as larger churches do, if not more. It is just that the rules are often unspoken and unwritten (and protected by mavens). Some might even say that informal norms ("church politics") keep small churches small. And community can be fostered in the larger church as well, but on the model of the "two-pizza rule" said to be in force at the online retailer Amazon (the rule says that if a team can't be fed with two pizzas, the team is too big and will bog down in bureaucracy).

Living in a smaller community naturally tends to expose you to fewer ideas, opinions, and options, and this can be both a good thing and a bad thing. Small communities can prove to be both sheltering and too sheltering. People in smaller communities are not exposed to the same range of possibilities that exists in larger urban centers. For instance, major motion pictures are viewed in theaters in major markets and only get to small towns via DVD months later. Because studios have determined that movies need an audience of 1,500 or more viewers in the first two weeks, there are not many first-run films being shown in small towns. Because booksellers have determined that a bookstore needs to turn over every book on its shelves four times a year, there is not nearly the selection in a smaller community that you might find in a metropolitan area. In smaller communities, for example, many shops will not be set up because they cannot generate sufficient demand to earn their keep. Of course, with the booming Internet and shipping services such as UPS and FedEx, many items can now be purchased online and delivered to rural communities, but this eliminates the personal touch of interacting with the shopkeeper. So in some cases, the smaller community proves less personal than the larger urban center, where every purchase is a personal exchange, and there are a lot of these exchanges taking place every day.

Because small markets are small by definition, the organizations that serve them must be able to be profitable on a smaller scale. This is particularly challenging to the American church, where the expectation of full-time clergy is ingrained. Biblical solutions exist, such as volunteer ministry and tent making, but the "late" church has been slower than the early church was to adopt bivocational solutions.

Small groups can also sometimes think *too* small when it comes to meeting needs. True, there are not the amassed resources in a microchurch that there may be in a megachurch. But there was a degree of devotion and sacrifice in first-century Christian gatherings that is often missing in today's microchurches. Participants in the early church sold their possessions and goods and gave to those in need. Significant needs were met through the sacrifice of the cell. In truth, there are few needs that the microchurch cannot meet as well as the megachurch if the microchurch's participants are willing to sacrifice.

I have long wanted CTK be an "Acts 2" church. In many respects, we are. But one phrase that haunts us is the one about selling our possessions and goods. We haven't done a lot of that, although we have executed the "100-Thing Challenge" and "The Great CTK Giveaway" in some of our Worship Centers. There is a degree of radicalism in Acts 2 which we have not yet attained. It's not that we aren't meeting needs, but we are meeting needs at little cost to ourselves. The modern church tends to take a small amount of money from many people and use those funds to meet needs as they arise in the body (needs for housing, food, and so on). This needs-meeting model calls for a little bit from many. We can all feel good and feel no pain. But those same needs could be met in a smaller community if that community were to give to the point of sacrifice (a lot from a few).

The microchurch does not have to settle for having a micro-impact. Small groups can perform astounding feats that turn the world upside down. The desire to transform the spiritual landscape is anything but small. Osama bin Ladin executed an attack on the United States with nineteen cohorts and a total budget of around $400,000, but the results set the whole world reeling.

Elephant-Mouse Dynamics

Regardless of the size of our ministry assignments, we all have to give an account to our Master when He returns. C. H. Spurgeon was a megachurch pastor long before there was such a thing. His London congregation numbered five thousand at a time when such size was unheard of. Spurgeon recounted a story of meeting another minister of the day and asking him how many people attended his church. His colleague said, "About one hundred," to which Spurgeon replied, "I think that is enough to give an account on the Day of Judgment." No matter what size group God has called us to—megachurch, house fellowship, or small group—we are responsible to God to care for the needs of that group, with all its ups and downs.

I once received a visit from a church planting director of a major denomination at my office in Burlington, Washington. He wanted to get my recommendations about cities in Washington State that might be favorable for church planting. On his list were ten cities, and, as near as I could tell, it was a list of the ten most populated cities in the state: Seattle, Tacoma, Federal Way, Spokane, and so on. I looked over his list, handed it back, and said, "Yup. All of those could use a fresh expression of Christ." But then I added, without much pause, "But, then again, I think that every town in the state could use a fresh expression of Christ, so I wouldn't stop with this list." He gave me a puzzled look, followed by an awkward smile. I couldn't help myself. I was not in the mood for political correctness. I get frustrated when church planting organizations are not really looking for a town that needs a church. They are looking for a town with the population and money to support a church—and a large one, one that can grow and be viewed as "successful." I hope I don't sound too cynical here, and I hope that I'm wrong. But if I'm wrong, I'm not sure why there are not towns of under ten thousand people on the lists of church planting organizations. There are three hundred thousand Protestant churches in America, and most of them are relatively small (see Table 2.2).

Table 2.2. Percentage of Churches Based on Attendance

Weekly Attendance	Protestant Churches
1–99	177,000 (59%)
100–499	105,000 (35%)
500–999	12,000 (4%)
1,000–1,999	6,000 (2%)
2,000–9,999	1,170 (0.4%)
10,000+	40 (0.01%)

There are a few things that we can learn from Table 2.2. First, the majority of churches in America are not mega-churches: 94 percent have fewer than five hundred, and 98 percent have fewer than one thousand.

Second, the distribution of churches by size is similar to that identified by scientists who study fractals in the natural world. According to Ward, "Small clouds are common, medium-sized ones less so, and large clouds are rare. There is, however, a characteristic ratio at work that dictates the number of large versus small clouds."[20] This ratio is called a *power law*. A power law is a mathematician's term for talking about how one measure (here, the number of churches) can be expressed as a power of another measure (here, the size of the churches).

Third, extremely large churches are scarce. In the mentality of our culture, something that is scarce can seem to be in great demand, and therefore popular. But big does not equal great, nor does great equal big. The size of an animal is partly determined by the ability of the environment to support it. The plains were perfectly suited for the buffalo, since buffalo herds require an extravagantly spacious habitat to support themselves. Elephants are also of this ilk. Similarly, the largest churches in America are in the wealthy suburbs of major cities (see Table 2.3).

The average household income for the communities in which these churches are located is $84,600. The megamodel requires megabucks. The average size of the communities of the ten largest churches in America is nearly 1.6 million, a figure that uses the smaller size of the suburbs instead of their major metropolitan areas (for example, South Barrington, with a population of 4,461, instead of Chicago).

So if you live in a community like mine—Burlington, Washington (population 8,700, household income $47,000)—don't expect a megachurch to be coming to town anytime soon. Neither the population nor the economics can support it. But in God's economy, every person is an object of love and deserves

Table 2.3. The Ten Largest Churches in America in 2008

Name of Church	Size of Congregation	Suburb/City	Local Population	Average Household Income of the Community
1. Lakewood Church	43,500	Houston	2,200,000	$61,000
2. Second Baptist Church	23,659	Houston	2,200,000	$61,000
3. North Point Community Church	22,557	Alpharetta/ Atlanta	137,000	$94,000
4. Willow Creek Community Church	22,500	South Barrington/ Chicago	4,461	$203,000
5. LifeChurch.tv	20,823	Edmond/ Oklahoma City	80,000	$69,000
6. West Angeles Church of God in Christ	20,000	Los Angeles	9,800,000	$69,000
7. Fellowship Church	19,913	Grapevine/ Dallas	50,000	$87,000
8. Saddleback Church	19,414	Lake Forest/ Los Angeles	62,000	$84,000
9. Calvary Chapel	18,000	Fort Lauderdale	154,000	$77,000
10. The Potter's House	17,000	Dallas	1,279,000	$41,000

to be reached. This is where the smaller church comes in. Big churches can reach out in big communities, and in big ways; small churches can reach out in small communities, in small ways.

3

THE BEAUTY OF BOTH/AND

Can mice learn to leave a bigger footprint? Can elephants learn to be nimble on their feet? What if the mouse and the elephant worked together? What if the mouse could ride on the elephant's back? What if a thousand mice collaborated to lift an elephant? If elephants and mice could collaborate, it would seem that we would want them to.

It is a powerful thing to bring together two extremes. Canabou says that people "love the originality of small companies on a mission. Yet they also want economies of scale and a global footprint."[1] People want to reap the benefits of bigness and smallness simultaneously. They are drawn to organizations that can provide a personal touch and the simultaneous ability to project significant firepower. In the hybrid church, the potential exists to reach elephantine numbers of people while convening in mouselike clusters.

An advertisement I saw for an investment company captured the combination with a headline: "We're David and Goliath." It invited customers to take advantage of the company's size and agility. The ad went on to talk about the number of analysts the company had in its research department, evidently one of the largest in the industry. Then the ad spoke of the company's smaller working groups, which were devoted to particular sectors and regions. The punchline was that bigger plus smaller equals better.

To be both—bigger and smaller—is better. This holistic paradigm is captured in the words of an ancient Eastern proverb: "You think that because you understand *one*, you must understand *two*, because one and one make two. But you must also understand *and.*" Is it better to be bigger, or smaller? It is best to be both at the same time.

This craving for both/*and* may actually be hardwired into us, a reflection of the image of God. As the Psalmist says (Psalm 62:11–12):

> One thing God has spoken,
> Two things have I heard:
> That you, O God, are strong,
> And that you, O Lord, are loving.

God is both strong and loving. God is "and." I wouldn't be inclined to take my theology from George Burns, but in the film *Oh God, Book II*, a little girl asks Burns, playing the part of God, why bad things happen. God's response is to say that the system works that way: wherever there is an up, there is a down; there is always a top with a bottom, a front with a back. God then discloses that he can't take away sad without taking away happy, too. Then he coyly says that anyone who has a better idea should put it in the suggestion box.

One of the ways to verify the validity of a proposition is to look at its opposite. How well do things work out when we have imbalance? Does imbalance work in our diets, our families, our work lives? How about when you get an ear infection and it affects your balance—is your life better or worse? How about if you eat a diet of only carbohydrates? Do you feel better, or more sluggish?

One of the things I like about our mission statement at CTK is its sense of balance.

> Our mission: To create an authentic Christian community that effectively reaches out to unchurched people with love, acceptance, and forgiveness so that they may experience the joy of salvation and a purposeful life of discipleship.

Our mission statement defines who we want to be and what we want to do. It calls for us be an authentic Christian community that effectively reaches out. It balances community with outreach. Toward the end, our mission statement says that we want people to experience "the joy of salvation and a purposeful life of discipleship." I think that the reality behind these phrases is tough to actually execute, and we see differing nuances based on the gifts and graces that God places in the body, but these are worthy goals that take us in the right directions (and please note the plural).

We want to *be* something (an authentic Christian community) before we *do* something (effectively reach out). We want to be what Jesus wants us to be, and to do what Jesus wants us to do. It is out of a sense of community that we invite others to join us (1 John 1:1–4). As F. Scott Fitzgerald famously said in *The Crack-Up*, "The test of a first-rate intelligence is the ability to hold two opposed ideas in the mind at the same time, and still retain the ability to function." I think there will always be a tension between being and doing, and my thinking is that we don't want to choose one over the other. I wouldn't say that we've arrived at a perfect balance, or that, short of heaven, we will arrive at a perfect balance.

The key word in our mission statement is the relative pronoun *that* ("an authentic Christian community *that* effectively reaches out to unchurched people"). It is possible to be a Christian community and yet not reach out to others. It is also possible to be an outreach church and lose your sense of authentic Christian community. Our mission statement avoids both dangers.

If a church is not intentional about reaching out, Christian community can easily become an end in itself instead of a means to an end. Our mission holds us accountable for not letting this happen. I once had a lady take exception to CTK's emphasis on effectively reaching out to unchurched people. She said, "The church is for believers, not unbelievers." I had to disagree. The church is not *for* believers. It *is* believers. The church (ecclesia, derived from Greek *ekklēsiastēs*, an assembly of "called out ones") is who we are. But to say that the church is "for" us (as in "intended for" us) is to say that God has called us out for our own sake. This is circular thinking and contrary to Christ's marching orders to make disciples of all nations (Matthew 28:19, 20).

Poles and Spectrum

The mascot for all things Hybrid is the battery. The battery has two poles and is dead until you connect the positive to the negative charge. But it is a powerful, beautiful thing to bring extremes together, as you do when you combine creatives and analyticals, linear and nonlinear thinkers, right-brained and left-brained.

In nature you often see dualities. For instance, there are two eyes, two ears, two arms, two legs, two genders. For the globe, there is a north pole and a south pole, and there are day and night. In church life as well you see two poles toward which there is magnetic attraction.

Churches typically find themselves gravitating toward one pole or the other, from extremely intimate (Strongly N), at one end, to extremely impacting (Strongly M), at the other (see Figure 3.1).

Figure 3.1 Intimacy-to-Impact Spectrum

Strongly N ← → Strongly M

Intimate ← → Impacting

Exploring the interplay of intimacy and impact, I am reminded of the story of Mary, Martha, and Jesus recorded in Luke 10. Martha is busy in the kitchen, preparing a meal for her VIP, Jesus. Mary is sitting attentively at the feet of Jesus. Buchanan picks up the story:

Martha wrestles the crockery, thickens the sauce, bastes the lamb chops, sets the table. Mary is oblivious, dreamy and serene, even though Martha is sending up smoke signals thick and menacing. She places the tableware with an emphatic *clunk*. She raps the ladle on the pot's edge hard as a blacksmith nailing horseshoes. She sighs with a hiss like fire brazing water.

Still Mary doesn't notice.

So the lid finally boils over. Martha vents her frustration on both Jesus and Mary: "Lord, don't you care that my sister has left me to do the work by myself? Tell her to help me!" (Luke 10:40).

Jesus gently chides Martha, gently commends Mary. But it's his praise of Mary that should give us pause: "Mary has chosen what is better" (v. 42).

Mary's choice is only *better*.

What would be *best*?

My guess: Martha's industry joined to Mary's attentiveness. Martha's briskness and energy and diligence stemming from Mary's quietness and restfulness and vigilance. The best is to have Martha's hands and Mary's heart.[2]

I like that. I like that on a personal level and on a corporate level. The church experiences its greatest leverage by combining the best of Mary with the best of Martha. Heart and hands. Industry and attentiveness. Other contrasting words could be used to identify these terminals, such as the terms listed in Table 3.1.

I don't see any reason to pick sides. Jesus said there are two great commands, not one—love God with all your heart, soul, mind and strength, and love your neighbor as yourself. In fact, it is impossible to fulfill one of these commands without fulfilling the other. The first commandment, to love God, takes us deeper. The second commandment, to love others, takes us wider.

Table 3.1 Mega/Micro Contrast

Micro	Mega
Mouse	Elephant
Cell	Celebration
Personal	Powerful
Relational	Attractional
Organic	Organizational
Fast	Vast
Network	Mainframe
Informal	Formal
Bottom-up	Top-down
Family room	Living room
Improvisational	Scripted
Amateur	Professional
Decentralized	Centralized
Guerrilla	Conventional
High-touch	High-tech
Groups	Programs

There is no necessary contradiction between being Christlike and reaching out.

When it comes to intimacy and impact, as already mentioned, churches tend to find themselves at one pole of the spectrum (Strongly N) or the other (Strongly M). In between, of course, are shades of both, as is also the case in nature when it comes to opposites (see Figure 3.2).

In Figure 3.2, as with the five fingers of the human hand, between the outlying pinky finger and thumb of intimacy and impact are the three fingers of closeness, connectedness, and engagement. Intimate groups certainly can embark on formidable campaigns, just as churches of impact can emphasize intimate relationships. In general, however, each ministry has a discernible "vibe."

Stereotypes tend to give us simplistic, all-or-nothing categories. More often than we tend to realize, however, people live in a world with a plenitude of shades of gray. With respect to gender, for example, what appears at first glance to be a set of only two possibilities, male or female, appears more gradated when you realize that within each gender there is a range, from very masculine to effeminate in men and from very masculine to very feminine in women. And all that is without the curve balls that genetics can throw us, such as when people are born with both male and female organs. The point is that life is not always binary, not always 1 or 0, but often .7 and .2 or .53. Life can have more in common with a dimmer switch than with an on/off switch. Variations on themes are as diverse and as complicated as people (see Table 3.2).

Figure 3.2 Ethos of the Spectrum

Strongly N ← N   ← N/M   → M   → Strongly M

Intimate   ← Close ← Connected → Engaged → Impacting

Table 3.2 The Spectrum Relative to Size

	Strongly N	*N*	*N/M*	*M*	*Strongly M*
Vibe of Ministry	Intimate	Close	Connected	Engaged	Impacting
Description of Congregation	Microchurch	Small church	Medium-size church	Large church	Megachurch
Size of Congregation	<35	35–75	75–200	200–800	>800

The size groupings shown in Table 3.2 range from the cellular to the more conventional, and the numerical correlations are approximate, not fixed. The descriptors follow common church parlance, but I have chosen the term *microchurch* instead of *tiny church* or *extra-small church* because *microchurch* carries less negative baggage and, lately, conveys the sense of "boutique" (as in microbrews, microfinance, and so on).

No doubt there are some medium-size churches that are experiencing more intimacy than some small churches are (and those small churches may be small because there is no intimacy), and there are some small churches that are making a greater impact than some large churches are (and the large churches may be living off yesterday's accomplishments). But there is a general correlation between smallness and intimacy, and between bigness and impact. In Table 3.3, I have assigned a positive numerical value to each type of church across the spectrum, with increasing values for extremity in degrees of intimacy, impact, or some combination of the two. Both ends of the spectrum represent qualities that are desirable. The maximum value would be 6, for a church that is extremely intimate as well as extremely impacting.

Table 3.3 Value Designations Across the Spectrum

	Strongly N	*N*	*N/M*	*M*	*Strongly M*
Vibe of Ministry	Intimate	Close	Connected	Engaged	Impacting
Description of Congregation	Microchurch	Small church	Medium-size church	Large church	Megachurch
Size of Congregation	<35	35–75	75–200	200–800	800
Value	3	2	1	2	3

Of course, people and groups do express a range of motion; they are not static but dynamic. Small churches do things that are attractional, and large churches do things that are personal. Churches can even bounce from pole to pole, at times being more organizationally oriented, only to swing back to being more relationally oriented. There are even times when imbalance is balance, as when a short-term focus contributes to the overall mission. A mother with a new baby, for example, will spend an inordinate amount of time caring for the baby, and for a period of time her life will not be in balance. That limited-duration, front-loaded investment, however, is contextualized over the course of the child's life. Imbalance for a period of time contributes to balance overall. The goal for the hybrid church is to bring sustained emphasis to both.

Reach and Range

The middle ground represented by the word *connected* (see Tables 3.2, 3.3, and 3.4) is a watershed between two worlds. By *connected* we mean both relationally connected (looking to the left of the spectrum) and connected in terms of mission

Table 3.4 Desirability Across the Spectrum

	Strongly N *Best*	*N* *Better*	← → *N/M* *Good*	*M* *Better*	*Strongly M* *Best*
Vibe of Ministry	Intimate	Close	Connected	Engaged	Impacting
Description of Congregation	Micro	Small	Medium	Large	Mega
Size of Congregation	<35	35–75	75–200	200–800	>800
Value	3	2	1	2	3

(looking to the right). A church that occupies the Connected spot on the spectrum is in a liminal space, with a modicum of intimacy and impact. This does not mean, however, that this is the ideal place, or that a medium-size church that is able to bring elements of intimacy and impact does not need to make adjustments. Churches in the middle three sections of the spectrum have less radical adjustments to make to achieve balance than do those on either end, but they have to make adjustments in both directions to achieve better reach, as indicated by the bidirectional arrows in Table 3.4. The church at the Connected point on the spectrum may actually have significant work to do in order to move in both directions and become more extreme.

The balance we are searching for is balance by extremes. The broader, the better. A church with a range of Strongly N to Strongly M has a more formidable ministry than one that ranges from N/M to M. If you can envision straddling a teeter-totter, the ideal is to spread your legs as wide as possible instead of standing in the center above the fulcrum. Churches that have been polar (Strongly N or Strongly M) may have significant stretching to do in order to achieve greater reach. There are four degrees of separation between Strongly N and Strongly M. The distance between N and M is two degrees of separation. Groups that are either entirely intimate or highly attractional may need a major overhaul to create structures that range to the other end of the spectrum.

The goal for the hybrid church would be to have the longest possible reach and the broadest possible range. The term *reach* is used here to mean movement from the middle toward the edges, and the term *range* is used to mean movement that encompasses both sides of the spectrum. Churches with greater reach are becoming more extreme in their delivery of either intimacy or impact. These churches score higher than those in the middle of the spectrum. Churches with greater range are more intentional in their simultaneous delivery of intimacy and impact.

These churches score higher by gaining points from both ends of the spectrum.

Reach and range move us away from two less attractive possibilities—a church of moderation (not particularly notable for either intimacy or impact) and a church of imbalance (clearly on one side of the spectrum instead of on both). Reach pushes us toward greater intentionality in the ministry that reflects our comfort zone, and range takes us out of our comfort zone and moves us toward greater balance.

The most notable technological innovation of the new millennium, and one that expresses the ideas of both reach and range, is the Apple iPhone. The tech industry is finding synergy in the nexus of performance and portability. The best of both worlds is to have a supercomputer in your pocket—gadgetry that's grand—and the iPhone is the epitome of that.

Truly, Apple has done a marvelous job marketing the iPhone. But it's the both/and of performance and portability that has made the iPhone a sensation. Phones small enough to fit in one's pocket are ubiquitous. Nothing special there, if that's all that the iPhone represents. But that is not all. It also represents significant computing power, running a full Web browser and thousands of applications. There are tens of thousands of apps designed for the iPhone, with more than 1,600 apps for business use alone, including software from FedEx and accounting sites like Mint.com. Some businesses are now running their entire business on their phones.

Each iteration of the iPhone—following the trajectory of the iPod, the wildly popular portable music player that preceded it—has packed even more punch, in an ever-elegant case. The Internet backbone of the handset is well suited to deliver the value propositions of both immediacy and depth. With a few clicks on a touch screen, you can have information at your fingertips, and you can go as deep in your search as you want.

As the church moves into a hybrid world, it is that variety that we will be seeing and seeking. I've already mentioned my idea of sixty-second sermons (see Chapter Two). At the same time, as I look at my congregation I am realizing that there is a need for thorough, systematic indoctrination. At the rate some of the participants are taking in truth, they will forever be anemic in their faith. So I am coming back to the value of mid-week Bible classes and all-day Saturday seminars. At times, less is more. At other times, more is more.

A story that was reported to me by one of our CTK pastors illustrates the both/and nature and context of today's ministry. It is the story of a man who, one night a week, does something unusual to reach his neighbors. He fills an ice chest with beers, rolls up his garage door, turns on his propane patio-heater, sets out a circle of chairs, and invites guys to come over for a drink after work. It is not a Bible-study group by any means. It is bridge activity. Over time, this neighborhood hangout has grown in popularity so that now nearly all the men in the neighborhood look forward to it. It has become this man's ministry to build relationships. He decided he needed to do something much more aggressive to reach his neighbors for Christ.

At the same time, this man is also involved each week in hardcore Bible study, where he can strengthen his faith. Even as he is reaching out quite intentionally, he feels an even greater need for godliness. So he does both—the beer ministry on one night, the deeper Bible study on another. This is different from the old days, when we might have had a simple Bible study in our homes and then tried to invite our neighbors. In today's hybrid world, we need to be more relationally and biblically extraordinary than that. This story of balanced extremes is instructive to the entire church, in my opinion. We need to move swiftly to the edges.

4

THE EMERGING BLENDS

Because hybrid vehicles are more ecologically friendly than gas-combustion vehicles, hybrid technology is sometimes referred to as "green" technology. This is apropos, since yellow and blue make green. In a similar way, I would say that if yellow represents the personal intimacy of the church, and blue represents the powerful impact of the church, then we want to see green in the church as well.

How do churches become green? Not all in the same way. At times a hybrid may resemble a banana split (flavors kept separate but presented together), and at other times it may resemble a banana shake (flavors blended together). At times a hybrid may resemble stripes (alternating emphasis), and at other times it may resemble polka dots (a prevailing emphasis, with contrasting spots).

In transportation, hybridity is a trial-and-error, experimental world of varying shades and combinations. President Obama has a goal to have one million hybrid cars on the road by 2015. To encourage this goal, the Department of Energy is disbursing $25 billion in low-interest loans to encourage companies to build ecologically friendly vehicles. Both Honda and Toyota are responding to the challenge. But in an effort to generate market demand, they are developing hybrid cars with different formulations. While Toyota has the market-leading Prius, which is an electric vehicle with gas assist, Honda is now developing a mild hybrid offering, to be built on its Fit platform. The Honda Hybrid (Hh) is a departure from the company's original hybrid offering, the gas-electric Insight, a light two-seater that broke gas economy records (over seventy miles per gallon), but not sales records. The lackluster response to the Insight caused Honda to follow up with hybrid versions of its popular Civic and Accord lines. These were also modestly received by consumers, partly because the gas versions of these vehicles are relatively economical already.

With its upcoming third-generation hybrid, Honda believes it has stumbled upon the right formulation of performance and economy. Whereas the Insight yielded superior economy and higher cost than the Prius, the new Hh comes in at slightly lower cost (estimated $3,000 less than the Prius) and slightly less fuel economy (projected to be a few miles per gallon less than the Prius's fifty miles per gallon). Honda's Integrated Motor Assist technology essentially negates electric-only drive, so there will be no sneaking up on unsuspecting blind pedestrians. But the power plant will deliver consistent performance, something the company believes its target audience desires.

So while Honda is moving back toward greater reliance on its efficient gas engines, Toyota is moving more toward a plug-in version of its electric-focused Prius. Toyota plans to sell nearly five hundred thousand of its hybrid models each year, while Honda is setting production of its keenly priced Hh at two hundred thousand. The winner in all this? The consumer, who is finding options across the spectrum from gas to electric, from greater performance to greater economy.

In the up-and-coming world of the hybrid church, there is unprecedented experimentation in the blending of intimacy and impact. A discernible gravitational pull is obviously taking large churches in the direction of the microchurch, and vice versa. Large churches are exploring various ways in which they can break things down for greater community life. Small networks are looking for ways to gang up for greater visibility and influence.

Hybrid mixes range from the cellular to the conventional. So far, three "green" hybrid church blends are emerging along the spectrum of color that runs between yellow and blue: the association, the network, and the satellite (see Figure 4.1).

Figure 4.1. The Hybrid Color Spectrum

Yellow	Yellow Green	Green	Bluish Green	Blue
Micros	Associations	Networks	Satellites	Megas
	Cellular	Congregational	Celebrational	

Each of these shades of green provides some combination of intimacy and impact.

We'll explore the benefits of each approach, but first I want to share an overview of the CTK story, as I have affectionately called it, which has made stops across the spectrum.

A Green Church

The hybrid story with which I am associated, that of Christ the King Community Church, includes elements of all three hybrid models—association, network, and satellite. In some phases of our story we have functioned as a cellular association, in other phases we have been a congregational network, and in still other phases we have developed broadcast satellites. The CTK story is about the journey of a church group that, over a twenty-year period, went from being a small, single-cell congregation to a "green" network.

CTK began as a small church pastored by Steve Mason in Whatcom County, in the northwest corner of Washington State. In the early 1990s, I came to know about CTK as I was pastoring a traditional denominational church in a neighboring town about ten miles away. My church was larger and much more established, but it was growing only incrementally, primarily through transfers. CTK was smaller, but it was growing exponentially, primarily through conversions. One time I ran into Steve Mason at a wedding and asked him what explained the rapid growth of his church. His reply was pointed: "Church growth principles." Later I found out what some of those principles were.

Figure 4.2. The Intimacy-Impact Grid

	Intimacy	Impact
Small Groups	Personal	Powerful
Worship	Private	Public
Outreach	Relational	Attractional

Before Steve Mason even agreed to pastor the group that would become CTK, he had a few stipulations. He asked the group of fifty adults, before voting on him as pastor, to make a commitment that the church would focus its energies on only three things: worship, small groups, and outreach. He asked them to agree that the church would be a worshipping church (a church whose members would worship God as a lifestyle), a church centered on small-group ministry (as the primary way in which it would care for people and carry out the "one another" commands of scripture), and a church committed to outreach (caring intently about those who were about to come). The people made the deal—they literally signed on the dotted line— and the rest, as they say, is history. CTK's contrasting dynamics of intimacy and impact are illustrated in Figure 4.2.

Hardwired into the DNA of CTK from the beginning was a value proposition that incorporated intimacy and impact. CTK met in small as well as larger gatherings. The primary gathering size of our church is the small-group meeting that takes place during the week in a living room or a restaurant. It is three to ten people gathered in Jesus' name for friendship, growth, encouragement, and outreach. A secondary convention for our church is what we call a Worship Center—a larger corporate gathering of thirty to three thousand people for worship, teaching, and prayer. This is a meeting that takes place in a rented public facility, such as a school, a hall, or a community center.

Throughout the history of CTK we have seen the cell (the small group) and celebration (the Worship Center) play off

Table 4.1. CTK Attendance, Early 1990s

Year	Attendance
1988	71
1989	94
1990	131
1991	244
1992	306
1993	487

each other. Small groups are a side door into the church. The weekend worship is a front door into the church. Some people are attracted by the small fellowships and then find their way into the public worship service; others are attracted by the large public gatherings, and we try to funnel them into a small group. This synergetic approach yielded rapid growth in the early 1990s (see Table 4.1).

Through the mid-1990s, CTK was in the early stages of developing multiple worship teams and services, eventually meeting at two different locations. One was the original site, a smaller church building in Laurel, Washington, about ten miles north of Bellingham. The other was a converted warehouse on the north edge of Bellingham. It was during this period that I joined the staff of the church as associate pastor and campus pastor for the group meeting in Laurel. For a couple of years, services were held at both locations and were "stagger started" at forty-five-minute intervals to allow the worship teams and teachers enough time to drive between locations. We would often pass each other going from location to location. It was a chaotic, crazy, exhilarating time, but people were being led to Christ and baptized. The church was growing rapidly (see Table 4.2). Our growth defied explanation. It was a "God thing."

Toward the end of this period of rapid growth, I put forward a proposal to the other leaders of CTK. The idea was to develop

Table 4.2. CTK Attendance, Late 1990s

Year	Attendance
1994	673
1995	1007
1996	1380
1997	1758
1998	2190
1999	2405

a third location in order to accommodate continued growth. I started with the question that was on everyone's mind: "Where do we go from here?"

This is a question that has been asked before and, Lord willing, will be asked again many times. But because of the significant attendance benchmark that we are at (2,000), and the potential for future outreach that is on the horizon, how we answer the question at this juncture is particularly significant. The question may be refined to ask, "How can we continue to accommodate growing numbers of worshipers at our weekend celebrations as we continue to build our small-group network?" Initial answers to this question could run down two main tracks: bigger or more. Either we find a bigger container to hold more people or more containers to hold more people. Each paradigm carries its own set of possibilities.

Following are some thoughts on the more unconventional of the two tracks: developing more venues for more people to convene for worship. For lack of a better designation, I've chosen to call this the *chapel model*.

The big idea behind the chapel model is to continue to convene different worship services, at different times, in different locations, with different worship teams, and different preachers. Each of these venues would be a manifestation of the bigger entity, CTK.

I saw these chapels as a natural extension of our small-group philosophy, reinforcing our community feel and our growth-through-multiplication philosophy. I envisioned the decentralization of pastoral care, with some centralized administrative services, such as accounting, and some countywide cooperative ministries, such as counseling, children's ministry, and outreach events. I wasn't quite sure how all of this would work, but I had the broadest strokes figured out.

At the time, the other leaders involved in the CTK story didn't share my enthusiasm for the chapel model. We were already meeting in more than one place, but when I made my proposal, multisite churches were untested and novel (there were fewer than a hundred nationwide, compared to more than two thousand today). Meeting in multiple places seemed like an aberration rather than something that could be considered normal. But I think the bigger reason that my proposal was not adopted was that our leadership team was worn out from trying to keep up with years of 30 percent annual growth. Fatigue made consolidation particularly attractive. Bringing things together in one location would at least cut down on the running around we were doing.

Therefore, in 1997, Christ the King Community Church purchased an eighty-thousand-square-foot building on the north side of Bellingham and consolidated. Overnight we went from convening people by the hundreds, in several services, to convening them by the thousands, in a couple of services. I had a front-row seat to observe the trade-offs that come with increased scale. With our larger presence in the community, we began to draw more people through the front door than through the side door (our small groups). At the same time, our people began to be more passive, and soon much of the bottom-up nature of our ministry's activities ceased. Our people became content to leave things to the professionals.

In 1999, through a series of God-directed events, I was led to start a new location of CTK in neighboring Skagit County, in

the town of Mount Vernon, thirty minutes south of Bellingham.
I did not have a plan to start a church. I just happened to be
on the scene when God brought together about a hundred
Christian people who were all in search of a church home. They
asked if CTK could come south, and I was dispatched to help
them organize. Very quickly, this new venture took off.

During its first year, Christ the King of Skagit Valley grew at
a rate of 12 percent a month, until an average of more than 500
people were attending our church every week. The high attendance was 763 on Easter in 2000, the church's first anniver-
sary. By then, thirty-eight small groups were convening weekly
throughout the Skagit Valley.

As opportunities arose, we decided to say, "Yes, sure, you
bet" to expanding the ministry into additional communities
and counties. In October 2000, Christ the King began hold-
ing Saturday night services in Oak Harbor (twenty-five miles
southwest) and Anacortes (twenty miles west). We rented
school facilities to accommodate the growing numbers of people
traveling to these locations. During its second year, Christ the
King grew to more than fifty small groups meeting weekly, and
to a high attendance of 1,034 on the church's second birth-
day (on Easter in 2001). On July 15, 2001, CTK held its first
Sunday worship service in LaConner. In 2002, CTK opened
in Stanwood. In 2003, CTK launched Worship Centers in five
additional communities in four counties. In 2005, CTK began
to expand across the country and around the world and changed
its name from Christ the King of Skagit Valley to Christ the
King Community Church, International.

In all, there are more than twenty thousand participants in
our branch of the CTK story. As we move into new communities, we begin by forming small groups. Once we have two or
more groups meeting in any one area, we bring those groups
together in a Worship Center, as a convention of cells. It is a
blended approach that has served us well. The viral nature of our
small-group approach has allowed us to establish small groups

and Worship Centers across the United States and has taken CTK into thirty-two other countries around the world. In India, for example, there are now more than four hundred CTK groups, and on the continent of Africa there are more than a thousand.

Meanwhile, as CTK Skagit County has developed into a congregational network, CTK Bellingham has continued to grow as a megachurch (now with more than four thousand participants) and planted additional CTK sites in Blaine and Lynden. CTK Lynden, in turn, has also developed into a sizable congregation that has been instrumental in launching satellites in the nearby communities of Everson and Kendall. Most recently, CTK Bellingham has begun a video extension campus in Ferndale. Currently there are several branches of the CTK story that exemplify the different ways in which the church can meld intimacy and impact, across the color spectrum from yellow to blue.

Associations

On the celluar side of the spectrum is the association. Associations are typically smaller pieces joined together to make an impact, as in the cellular architecture of the Internet. They embrace the motto "You do big things by doing lots of small things."

Cellular associations obtain elements of intimacy and impact by being highly relational yet missionally connected. Some micronetworks see intimacy as the first objective, but some see disciple making as the first objective, with intimacy as a by-product. All cellular associations feel that it is important to bring people into a context where people are opening up their lives. What is certain is that in a small group it is easier to be transparent. Thinus Coetzee, the continental champion for CTK in Africa, says, "In Africa we've learned from the animals that there is safety in numbers. If there is no intimacy, the chance of going away—astray—is a great risk."

The associational hybrid includes house church networks and parachurch disciple-making organizations touting some of the leading thinkers of the contemporary church, such as Alan Hirsch, Tony Dale, Frank Viola, Hugh Halter, and Neil Cole. But Cole, uniquely, has not just espoused a cellular theory of the church; he has also put that theory into practice through his Church Multiplication Associates (CMA). Tony Dale, a microchurch expert and developer of the House2House Web site, calls CMA the most identifiable movement of the microchurch in America.

Neil Cole is the author of *Organic Church*, *Organic Leadership* and *Church 3.0*, in which he describes his innovative approach to church. The basic building block of his ministry is the Life Transformation Group (LTG) of two to three people. Someone who becomes a Christian becomes a participant in one of these Life Transformation Groups, where every week people confess sins, read scripture (thirty chapters a week), and make a list of unbelievers for whom they will be praying and reaching out.

CMA is commonly misunderstood to be a house church network. In fact, Cole advocates groups of different sizes for different dynamics, roughly basing his methods on Jesus' experiences from the Gospels—from intimacy with a core to public ministry to the masses. Cole says, "The smallest group of two to three is best for disciple making." The LTG roughly approximates Jesus' intimate relationship with James and John. Cole believes that the group of five to seven is best for a leadership team. The group of twelve to fifteen is best for a sense of family (Jesus' twelve disciples roughly approximating a house church); the group of twenty to seventy-five is best for training; the group of one hundred to one hundred twenty is the ideal size for a network (ten house churches); and the group of up to five hundred is best for communicating truth rapidly to a large group. But, as Cole is quick to say, with the larger groups "it was possible for Jesus to feed, teach, and heal, but not disciple."

The social architecture of CMA is more intentional than most people have realized. Cole cites Dunbar's number (one hundred fifty) as reflecting an important limitation in terms of effective relationships. (From the research of the British anthro-pologist Robin Dunbar it was discovered that most people, regardless of the context, cannot effectively maintain relation-ships in a group that exceeds one hundred fifty members.)

Cole sees both intimacy and impact in his story. He says, "That's two-thirds of our DNA." He uses the acronym DNA to stand for CMA's three-part value system of divine truth, nurturing relationships, and apostolic mission: "We achieve inti-macy through nurturing relationships, impact through apostolic mission." He does not see either intimacy or impact predominat-ing over the other. But with the primary emphasis on the LTG, the intimacy of the small group is certainly no small matter: "When we're openly confessing everything to everyone every week in a Life Transformation Group, it gets pretty trusting."

From the yellow-green perspective, intimacy takes place before impact. Coetzee compares this interrelationship to farming. "The farmer loves his land, his seed, and tends to it—that's intimacy. He can also picture the harvest—that's impact." The impact may take longer to materialize, but when the results come in, there will be better retention with a foundation of intimacy. "To draw people through impact, you need a lot of activities," Coetzee says. "If you have intimacy, it is organic. By keeping the intimacy constant, the risk of people leaving is nullified."

The impact Cole sees coming from his story starts with per-sonal efforts that participants make in sharing the Gospel with loved ones: "As people are ignited with the kingdom of God, they bring that with them into every area of society—their play, work, relationships." So the beginning point for the church's impact is personal, but that is only the beginning. The goal is to multiply disciples, leaders, churches, and movements. Just as "the DNA is in every disciple," it also needs to be "in relation-ship to every disciple." Disciples soon begin to coordinate their activities for greater impact. At times, LTGs come together as small congregations, particularly when they reach out to a social network. "We don't make it happen," Cole says, "but we do teach that it can happen."

In his book *Search and Rescue*, Cole enumerates seven different ways in which a Life Transformation Group can become an organic church:

1. LTGs can multiply and then come together in a separate place.
2. Members of an LTG can reach a large group of affiliated unbelievers in a chain reaction.
3. A church planting team can form for the purpose of planting a church, using LTGs as its strategy.
4. A group of people already organized in cells can break away from an established church.
5. A group of Christians hungry for a more authentic expression of faith can organize into LTGs.
6. A group of unbelievers coming to Christ can find out about LTGs.
7. A group of unchurched Christians in an area can come together for a new expression of faith.[1]

Over the years, CMA has seen all of these things happen. As groups have coalesced, Cole has been surprised by some of the nice things that have happened. In inner-city Long Beach, for example, some leaders from CMA went to start up some organic house churches. An African American woman named Dorcas opened up her home to the group, even though she was a Muslim, not a Christian. Initially, she was less than enamored with the group's teaching about Christ. In fact, on one occasion, when the participants spoke of Christ, she threw food at them. But over time she realized that they were taking their faith seriously, and she grew to respect that. She could see that they were earnestly reading their Bibles, seeking after God, and carrying out acts of kindness in the community. After a thorough investigation of Christianity, she converted. After her conversion, she started a food bank in her garage, and this is where collaboration and networking with other LTGs and house churches have become significant. Through the support of the greater community of believers, that food bank now feeds hundreds of people each week.

Cole is also at the forefront of conversations that are starting to happen between microchurch and megachurch leaders. "There's something going on," says Cole. He is seeing megachurches forming smaller missional communities and even releasing them to be separate from the megachurches. He is also seeing small groups with a greater desire to link up for purposes bigger than themselves. Tony Dale echoes, "There is a growing awareness that house churches should network, that an isolated house church is a vulnerable house church." He cites Web sites (such as Lk10.com) and CMA's Greenhouse events (which are open to anyone wanting to learn simple, organic principles) as fueling the fire of interconnectedness among house church practitioners.

One interesting development that may foreshadow future hybrid possibilities is that Neil Cole has been meeting regularly in the Los Angeles area with the influential pastors Dave Gibbons, Francis Chan, and Jaeson Ma. These have been bridge-building conversations that may or may not lead to cooperative efforts. Cole comments, "We haven't talked strategically about working together. We first have to make the relational connection. We have to trust each other. If we make it about plans and strategy, it will be short-lived." In an effort to deepen these relationships, they are planning to go with their wives on a short-term mission trip. Pressed about what the long-term strategic intent might be, Cole says that at this point he is praying that he and his colleagues "will realize that each of us has something that we all need, and we will all give of ourselves to the greater thing."

It's not hard to see what a powerful team the four of them could form. Neil is one of the foremost experts on organic discipleship and leader deployment, Jaeson is a leading cross-cultural evangelist, Dave is extremely connected to top-level influencers, and Francis is a gifted communicator with a huge number of people who listen to him. As examples of the synergies that could come, Neil has insights that could multiply the impact of Dave's contacts, Francis has a platform from which he could influence thousands regarding organic forms of church, and Jaeson has the savvy to coach Neil's network toward greater evangelistic effectiveness. "We are still in the conversation phase," says Neil, but the goal would be to "church L.A." As fast these guys move, I believe it won't take long before a hybrid form of church is unveiled in the Los Angeles area.

Austin, Texas, is another city where synergy is starting to develop. Megachurch Austin Stone Church started asking, "What if big churches begin to release people to start missional communities?" The church began to envision missional communities, small groups of people joined by the Gospel, pursuing the renewal and redemption of their community together. As the church began to explore these possibilities, fellowships were initiated with Tony and Felicity Dale, who lead a house church ministry based in Austin, and church participants were introduced to leaders of other missional communities across the country.

Right at that time, three microchurch networks—CMA, led by Neil Cole; Forge, led by Alan Hirsch; and Missio, led by Hugh Halter—were in discussions about putting on a national conference. But they realized that none of them had the centralized manpower or expertise to do so. This is where Austin Stone's size and strength came to the rescue. Austin Stone teamed up with fellow Austin multisite church Hill Country Bible Church to host the Verge Conference, with 2,500 registrants. Tony Dale understates the case: "The megachurch brings a lot to the table." Truly, the caliber of the people, the thinking, the money, and the media is extraordinary in most megachurches today. Dale says, "Large can market things in ways the small cannot even think about." In fact, small might even have a slight antagonism toward marketing.

The "think big" mantra of most megachurches, when tied to the "think small" mantra of the microchurches, creates some exciting possibilities. The small, when it goes viral, has extraordinary ability to touch people. As Orlando's Northland Church ("A Church Distributed") has deliberated about this potential, the church has been led to a "big, hairy, audacious goal," that of helping launch one million house churches in the coming years. I'm not sure whether that goal will be reached or not. But just the fact that the church thinks it might is an indicator of the tremendous possibilities latent in the hybrid church.

Those hybrid possibilities have an enemy, however—the suspicious, nontrusting, territorial thinking that is common to man and found even in the church. Hybrid forms require mutual trust and dependence. Ego works against this collaboration, and human nature is the same in the smaller context as in the big context. "There may not be the high press or salaries," says Neil Cole, "but jealousy and envy can be at work in the house church, too." One leader I spoke with mentioned an "inverted arrogance" that can attend the microchurch, where participants are proud of the fact that they are not big.

In South Africa, leaders are finding ways to get around barriers of pride and self-protection. CTK small groups in different regions are connecting with megachurches, often helping them start small groups. Megachurches are supporting the CTK story by offering facilities and credibility. "They are lending us the impact they already have," says Thinus Coetzee. "CTK shares what we know. Mega shares what they have." A simple question guides them in the relationship. They keep asking, "What would grace be in this instance—to share what I have with them, and they share what they have with me?" Coetzee sees it as a blessing for believers in the CTK story to supplement and complement established churches. "God blessed us with poverty. Why? Because we don't have big buildings, we have to rely on other churches."

Coetzee uses the cotton harvest as inspiration for how micro and mega can come together: "People come from all around to bring in the harvest." CTK Africa's message of brotherhood is important to unbelievers as well as to believers. In Zimbabwe, there are elders in the villages who have opened doors to some of our pastors in those villages because of their message of unity. Coetzee says, "The objective is to not have churches come together as different organizations but as one body." Associations show us that the hybrid church can be as simple as brothers coming together in unity.

Networks

Toward the middle of the spectrum are congregational networks. They cluster not just in small groups but in medium-size and larger groups. Among the models functioning this way are organic multisite churches like Xenos Christian Fellowship in Columbus, Ohio. Networks realize the best of both worlds by manifesting the house-to-house and temple courts combination of the first-century church.

Dennis McCallum is one of the soft-spoken founders of Xenos. When you ask him which word resonates more with him, intimacy or impact, he replies, "They are like two wings on an airplane. It's hard to say which is more important." This is a classic green response.

Xenos began in the early 1970s as an underground Christian newspaper called *The Fish*, distributed on the campus of Ohio State University. The newspaper sparked home studies (Fish House Fellowships), each with between fifteen and sixty members. As Xenos made the transition from one group to multiple groups, some participants expressed their unhappiness about not being able to hear key speakers, so Xenos began to offer larger meetings where the groups could share teaching (some of the meetings were on Sunday, but they were also held on weekday nights, and at different venues). To this day, the multihouse central meetings are mainly just straightforward teaching, and afterward the floor is opened to questions. Over the years, Xenos has grown to approximately five thousand members based out of three hundred house churches.

Because Xenos has more than two thousand people, the church is sometimes classified as a megachurch. But there are actually more people participating in small groups than in the large meetings. "From the outside, people see impact," says McCallum, "but from the inside, people see intimacy." McCallum dislikes the megachurch label because it is often associated with "an entertainment/celebrity approach." At the church's large-group gatherings, there are different teachers who are rotated so that no affinity develops for any one pastor.

Xenos is centered on lay leaders and house church activities. Leaders are trained and mentored to carry out the fifty "one another" passages in scripture. McCallum says, "Real relationships with people are more than just having a 'lovey' feeling with people when you see them in the lobby." McCallum sees relationships as foundational to both intimacy and impact. Much of the growth for Xenos has been through friendship evangelism. Xenos focuses on student ministry and has around one thousand college students either engaged in house churches or living in on-campus ministry houses.

McCallum feels that Xenos, as a network of house churches, is aptly described as a hybrid. Each of the house churches is involved in practical needs-meeting ministries in the community, such as programs serving inner-city and immigrant populations. Xenos was even singled out by President George H. W. Bush as one of the nation's leading "points of light" in community transformation for lauching Urban Concern. Whereas intimacy gives rise to impact from the association perspective, from the network perspective impact gives rise to intimacy.

In Philippians, Paul talks about being united in purpose. McCallum says, "The groups that are closest are 'on mission.' Having an impact is also part of building intimacy. A group that doesn't see itself as part of something bigger than itself starts to become boring and annoying. The shared purpose is what we're talking about, praying about, rejoicing about." Xenos is seeing more local, spontaneous service projects being launched "to adorn the Gospel." The church's teachers are speaking to the need to be purposeful in getting out in the community as a statement, as a testimony. Most feel it is working, leading to higher morale.

McCallum sees intimacy and impact giving rise to each other. Having an impact is helpful to building the intimacy of the group. Having intimacy is important to impact, especially for lasting fruit. He sees the pragmatism of the market-driven church mentality yielding poor results. "Churches have been tripping over each other to present the softest possible definition of what Christianity is," he says. "We have to hold out for the full New Testament picture."

The central teaching that Xenos carries out roughly approximates the temple courts meeting that we read about in Acts. Tony Dale, microchurch leader, doesn't see an ongoing role for a temple courts gathering, and this may be one of the distinctions between an association and a network. Dale feels that "the temple courts were just a natural gathering place, once thousands of people had found the Lord. But the church quickly moved into a house structure because of persecution, and stayed there. The temple courts didn't have an ongoing meaningful part to play for the next three hundred years." McCallum sees the Xenos model as more reminiscent of the church in Ephesus than the church in Jerusalem. In Ephesus, there were thousands of Christians convening in homes.

In the CTK story, particularly the branch that started in Mount Vernon, we have taken a both/and approach similar to that of Xenos. Our primary meeting is in the small group, but we have a secondary, weekly temple courts gathering as a convention of cells. Cliff Tadema, who now pastors CTK Mount Vernon (one of the larger Worship Centers of about one thousand), says that both intimacy and impact resonate with him, but "intimacy done right makes the greatest impact." Uncharacteristically for a large-church pastor, he says, "Intimacy requires authenticity, which leads to vulnerability, which leads to true fellowship, which is magnetic and ultimately leads to impact." When believers are authentically living life together, with God at the center, the church has a great impact on the community around it.

Toward this end, Tadema sees the value of both larger and smaller gatherings. Some need to see Christianity up close and personal, as they can in a small group. Others want to enter a larger environment incognito. Tadema feels that the culture has shifted to where people might be even more inclined to come to a larger church first instead of a small home setting, because it feels safer. He says, "They like to be able to hide out, so they can slide out." He goes on to say, "Of course, that is also the weakness of a larger church—people hiding out."

To combat that weakness, CTK Mount Vernon stresses the importance of relationships in its worship services. Tadema tries to connect the dots by offering prayer after every service. "We do it because of what it says as much as for what it does." The delivery of the message may be impacting, but the message itself is intimacy. Three recent sermon series that Tadema has taught are "Always a Place for You," "Better Together," and "Crazy Love." The feeling is that God has left us on Earth to grow in our relationship with Him and with others; we need to live interdependently, as a body.

As Tadema encounters individuals in his Worship Center, he is intentional about cultivating relationships by asking three questions:

1. Are you in a small group?
2. Are you in a relationship with someone?
3. How are you intentionally keeping Christ in the middle of your relationship?

He asks questions 2 and 3 because he does not assume that being in a small group automatically means experiencing authentic Christian community. He believes it is possible to be in a group and not be having meaningful, Christ-centered relationships. He also believes that it is possible to be having meaningful, Christ-centered relationships and not be in a small group. He is as big a fan of informal relationships as he is of formal relationships.

"Small groups are a vehicle, perhaps the best we know of," opines Tadema. But Tadema says CTK is less concerned about what a small group means and more concerned about the connections it facilitates. "Everyone is viewed as a minister and, if engaged in ministry, in need of support." The support needed for ministry doesn't have to be a lot, but it does have to be intentional, especially in a large church. As a green church leader, Tadema keeps both intimacy and impact in view. "Whatever one you think you want to lead with, you have to be intentional about the other one."

Satellites

On the right (bluish) side of the spectrum are satellite churches like Seacoast Church. Many megachurches like Seacoast are becoming multisite churches to accommodate the large numbers of people attracted to their ministries. Through satellite venues, they are achieving a higher level of intimacy by breaking the church down into subsidiary celebrations.

As an example of subsidiarity, Fraser Morrison owns a large construction business, but he split the business into family-size units, each with between thirty and sixty staff. He explains why:

That way they can get to know all of their people quite well. It's worked very well for us. A small operation just works better. The people enjoy it more and take a huge amount of satisfaction from it. You can get the team spirit, which is very important in construction. The same with commitment. I think it's in the small companies that you tend to find it. As we grow, it's a priority to make sure that we create the structure to be able to continually feel like a small company.[2]

Certain megachurches are leading boldly in this direction, some by serendipity. Seacoast went in this direction by necessity. Seacoast Church began in February of 1988 with sixty-five people meeting in an apartment clubhouse. Their dream was to build a church that would present the claims of Christianity in a contemporary fashion and allow nonbelievers to explore those claims at their own pace. The fledgling church held services in a rented theater, and then in an elementary school, until purchasing fourteen acres of property between Mt. Pleasant and North Charleston, South Carolina. The church built its first auditorium in 1991, experienced rapid growth through the 1990s, and later underwent several expansions on the property. The expansion plans eventually met resistance from Mount Pleasant's planning department, which began to see this large church as too large.

In 2002, Seacoast rented space in a nearby shopping center to host a video overflow service for young adults. The venue was dubbed the Annex. To the church's surprise, the off-site venue was very popular. Some even preferred the cozy Annex to the bigger "mother" church in Mt. Pleasant. The discovery led the church to establish video campuses in four other communities in the following year—downtown Charleston, West Ashley, Columbia, and Irmo. Seacoast has continued to expand in this manner, to the point where now most of the participants at Seacoast attend at video campuses, some even in other states.

Does Seacoast ever try to bring all of its campuses together for a larger celebration? The church did that early on but found it to be terribly costly, with logistical challenges, such as kids' ministry. "The staff loved it," says Geoff Surratt, Seacoast's ministry pastor along with his brother Greg, "but the people were so-so." Instead, the church has gravitated toward online leadership conferences as a way to keep the larger story united. And Surratt doesn't see a biblical precedent for getting the entire church together: "There were small groups and temple court gatherings, but they didn't try to get the entire church from different cities to come together."

Regarding intimacy and impact, Geoff says, "When I think of the 'big C' church, I think impact. I think worldwide missions." But he is quick to add, "At the same time, what is driving me is the intimacy part." Through expansion into multiple sites, the Seacoast leadership has seen the church's ministry become more missional and less attractional.

As the church has become closer to individual communities, it has also become more closely involved in those communities. In 2007, the church's North Charleston campus developed its Dream Center to provide medical and social services in the inner-city environment, and it is the church's expressed desire to see each of the campuses eventually take on these needs-meeting qualities, either through a Dream Center or through small groups that are adopting a block. Surratt likes the balance he sees emerging from this practical needs-meeting emphasis: "There is intimacy in the group, and yet in the blocks there is impact." Surratt now spends a lot of time helping small groups increase their impact through community enterprises.

There are also global enterprises for which the people of Seacoast are mobilized. At the end of 2009, Seacoast undertook the Hope Epidemic, a project to provide clean water for three hundred thousand people in two Third World countries. This project was under way prior to the devastating earthquake in Haiti, "so we were able to send clean water units to Haiti instantly." Seacoast tries to take advantage of its size by utilizing 28 percent of its resources for central support costs so that there is significant infrastructure available to respond as a larger church would when needs arise.

In the CTK story, we have also seen the benefit of meeting needs in the community. Kim Ryan, pastor of CTK Lynden (around two thousand people), says, "We're able to do so much more because there is so much more of us." He acknowledges that there are also more who are "not doing things," but, he says, "still there are more people doing things." When the disaster in Haiti struck, "we had a check for $10,000 out the door right away." Since then, the church has sent three containers of materials and supplies. This has created positive feelings all around. The non-Christian people in the community have expressed respect for the church—"We can't believe what you guys did for Haiti!"—and the congregation has rejoiced to hear of more than four hundred people coming to Christ through their efforts. Ryan likes the buzz going through the church. "It's good to be on a winning team," he says.

Closer to home, the Lynden group has a winning strategy of raising money to put new photocopiers in local schools and adopting classrooms through the school district. "The schools don't have the money," Ryan says. But he also sees the school projects as a means to "pastor the community" and "reframe people's perceptions" about the church.

The ability to mobilize significant resources, whether people or money, is one of the more obvious advantages of the megachurch over the microchurch. Tony Dale tells of an evangelist coming to Austin, Texas, and expecting to have a very large crusade, with fifteen thousand people or more expected to be in attendance in only six weeks' time. Knowing that Dale oversees an extensive house church network, the evangelist contacted him about providing discipleship support for the rallies. Dale was glad to help out, but he also contacted his friend Mike "Stew" Stewart at Austin Stone. "Stew would have more ability to do something quickly," Dale explains. "Trying to get house churches to work together is challenging, like herding cats." Most of the three hundred leaders Dale has deployed in house church ministry are not strictly identified with him as belonging to his House2House ministry. Even though Dale's informal network has experienced 200 percent growth in its groups over the years, Dale concedes that he "can't leverage it into anything . . . can't even track it." He has influence, but not control, over the network.

As Seacoast becomes known for its projects in community transformation, the church is continuing to lean into intimacy as "an insider deal . . . what we're trying to lead you toward," according to Geoff Surratt. Small groups are an emphasis in every weekend's message. They are not just a program in the church but are considered the essence of it, "whether you are on a campus of eighty or eight thousand," says Surratt. The church is also encouraging more contact among group participants between group meetings, taking some of the intimacy online through the City (a Facebook-like application developed by Mars Hill Church in Seattle and now marketed by Zondervan). The church is trying to help take groups from "We meet once a week" to "We have a safe place online to connect and share prayer requests."

But the greatest innovations in the Seacoast story, says Surratt, are coming around the midsize gatherings that the church offers in addition to its small groups and worship services. These gatherings are offered either as a breakdown of the big or as a collection of the small. Some of these groups are based on relationships, some are based on missions, and some have a discipleship element. The gatherings, which may meet infrequently, are proving particularly helpful for connecting people who do not have the time in their schedules to accommodate a weekly small-group commitment. But some of the midsize gatherings are groups that have outgrown a typical small-group size and now include thirty or more people, and this is encouraged.

Seacoast is also bringing a more communal feeling to its weekend services. Over the years, Seacoast's services have shifted from a seeker style to a style that is more personal and participatory. The majority of the singing now happens at the end of the service (after the teaching), and there are often stations for people to come to—to receive the Lord's supper or confess sins or experience community. The feeling, according to Surratt, is "The people on stage have done their job, and now you need to do your job." Surratt says the church's services are more participatory, less like sitting in an auditorium. In all of its venues, Seacoast has sacrificed seating capacity for more room for people to move around and respond.

Kim Ryan tries to set an example of intimacy in the public worship setting by sharing deeply from his own life. He says, "Our public presentation is not veneered, not hyped." Ryan has shared such personal details as being approached by a prostitute and handling that temptation. "That authenticity causes the group to feel much closer." Grant Fishbook pastors CTK Bellingham, the largest of the congregations in the CTK story, around four thousand people each weekend. He says trying to bring intimacy to a crowd is the biggest challenge. He attempts to make the weekend services more personal by wandering through the commons before and after services. He has constructed a pier platform that takes him closer to the audience when he teaches. The church uses colors and draperies to make the room seem smaller. Fishbook calls people by name from the platform. "We work hard to make a big church seem small," he says. "Unfortunately, that is all an illusion." Fishbook concedes that people want intimacy not just with the person in front also but "side to side."

Fishbook calls CTK Bellingham's size both its best and its worst attribute. He says that people can hide and heal, but they can also get lost. "There are only three degrees of separation between the people in our church and anyone in the country. The challenge is to get everyone's hand out to find out who people are." He sees impact as giving rise to intimacy. People hear about CTK because of its popularity. Fishbook tells of a local gas station attendant who has pointed many people to CTK Bellingham, usually with the same story: "I don't do church, but I've heard good things Christ the King. Turn at the porn shop.

They have blue signs." Fishbook laughs about more people find-ing their way to CTK from this man's "turn at the porn shop" directions than in any other way. But these warm vibes have been created by the many good deeds that CTKers have done in the community. Fishbook summarizes, "If I can have an impact on you—say, by loaning you a shovel—I might be able to have intimacy with you. With impact comes influence. They are intertwined."

He sees the size of CTK as something he wants to leverage to the salvation of many people, but he bemoans the fact that of hundreds of people baptized, only a small percentage of adults and a slightly larger percentage of children can be accounted for. He is challenged by the number of people who come to CTK from other churches, assuming that there must be health at CTK if it has grown to such size. Dennis McCallum of Xenos views these as worrisome trends; 90 percent of church growth, he says, "consists of transfers from other evangelical churches. We're not winning people in meaningful numbers." But Fishbook doesn't see this as dissimilar to the Gospel accounts of Jesus' own min-istry: "Jesus got brand recognition, and then Jesus singled them out in relationship."

The "brand recognition" wielded by CTK Bellingham is a megaresponsibility that Fishbook feels acutely, and he reminds himself that much is expected from the person to whom much is given. He wants to handle the gravitational pull that comes with being the biggest church in town, and he wants to do so with character. He knows that "crowds are contagious," but he is sobered that "a lot rides on the twenty-seven minutes" of the message. Like Seacoast, CTK Bellingham has begun creat-ing satellite venues where Fishbook's teaching can be heard in a smaller context. Fishbook understands how ministries need to be contextualized for different communities. He grew up on the prairies of Manitoba hearing the low-German phrase "Your sausage is different than mine"—that is, every community has its own community flavor, literally. Fishbook feels that these flavors create great opportunities for the church that is willing to think hybrid.

Fishbook is trying to learn everything he can about being a hybrid church. He preaches, "Don't wrap your hands around either intimacy or impact so tight. Open your hands. You'll let some stuff go, but you also allow God to put some new stuff in." Surratt says that every church should be working out the tension between intimacy and impact. He struggles relating to churches that are extreme on either end, what he calls "concert churches" at one end and, at the other, the groups that say, "We're small, we're intimate," as if that were all there is to be. For CTK Bellingham, Seacoast Church, and many other satellite megachurches, as the church gets bigger, it gets smaller all the time.

5

THE CONVERGENCE OF INTIMACY AND IMPACT

Once you are able to appreciate that the microchurch and mega-church movements are both born of God, you can see how the Author of those stories would be inclined to weave them together.

Whenever intimacy and impact converge, there is synergy. Synergy is a "buy two, get one free" proposition. If we bring together strong elements of intimacy and impact, we naturally get a third component—buzz. It is electrifying to a congregation when the ministry is both personal and powerful.

The vision that is present in the megachurch, combined with the devotion present in the microchurch, could change the world. Tony Dale believes that there is awesome potential latent in the microchurch, waiting to be drawn out: "If house churches became evangelistic, it would be dynamite!" In the megachurch there is also an attending dream born of the Spirit: "What if we could get all of these people connected to each other?" How do we do bring that synergy about? By trial and error.

The Challenge of Hybrid

The challenge of the hybrid church is for every ministry to get smaller and larger at the same time. It is about the small church thinking big, and the big church thinking small. It is about the church stretching itself and not settling for its current reach and range. This is a challenge for every ministry along the spectrum, from the smallest cell to the largest celebration.

For the microchurch, the question is "How are you going to make an impact?" There is no question that the microchurch is growing in popularity and population. But as long as the microchurch remains private, its impact on the culture will be negligible.

The house church can start to achieve greater influence simply by publicizing its existence. For instance, in the town where I live, Burlington, Washington, I'm sure there are house churches meeting, but I could not tell you where or when. If I wanted to point someone in their direction, I wouldn't know where to have the person go. Much has been made of postmodernism, but we still live in a modern world, with modern conveniences. One of those conveniences is being locatable. There is something to be said for the church that has a sign, a phone number, a Web site, and an e-mail address, if not an office and a building. We are to be in the world, just not of the world.

Going public may also involve some practical ministry in the community, such as cleaning the local park or adopting a school. Are we serving others or ourselves? This may end up being one of the more fundamental philosophical questions to discern whether our ministry approach is truly virtuous or not. In Kenya, CTK small groups engage in microbusiness, creating small business enterprises for the sake of widows in the community. At CTK in Durango, Colorado, CTKers staff the local food bank. In Burlington, Washington, CTKers have cleaned the restrooms of the downtown businesses. At CTK, we say that small groups do four things: they love, they learn, they do, and they decide. We include "do" as a reminder that we are to be Christ's hands and feet in this world, and that every small group should be light in the darkness.

Cells may also achieve greater influence by aligning with a more prominent local church or parachurch ministry. The mouse doesn't need to become an elephant if it can catch a ride. For microchurch leaders, it is about having the courage to think bigger and more interconnectedly. At CTK Durango (a house church), Pastor Chip Johnson has built alliances with larger churches in the community. Some CTKers actually attend a large adult Sunday school class at the local Baptist church before attending the home worship gathering at CTK. And this is encouraged. Last Easter, CTK Durango actually cancelled services and instead participated with some of the area churches in what they had planned. Chip's philosophy: "Why should we try to do something big on Easter, when the other churches in town are already doing it?" These alliances have proved rewarding in both directions. The relationships are collegial among the pastors. Chip has found mentorship among the established pastors, and the area pastors are able to lean on Chip for encouragement and counseling on how they can become more agile and organic.

In the early days of CTK Mount Vernon, we collaborated often with area churches in children's ministry. We did not have the resources to conduct a midweek kids' club, for instance. So we contacted the area churches and asked if they would mind if we promoted their midweek activities. Then we put together a brochure, which we distributed for years, that listed the area programs in which our kids could be involved as participants and our parents could be involved as volunteers. We didn't try to do everything. We stayed focused on our mission to be a small-group church.

And yet what the organic church has considered small has not been nearly small enough. When we have thought small, we have thought of the small group of seven to ten people. But the small group of seven to ten people is proving not to be intimate enough. Small is two or three. CTK's Kim Ryan concurs: "I'm thinking that small is better. Smaller than the small we thought. Under five. Three to four. One-on-one connection. Life coaching." This is a megachurch leader, but he is thinking smaller than many microchurch leaders: "I'm convinced that the group of ten doesn't work. People don't get together with the same real commitment. It dissipates to an unmeaningful time. We push 'small group' and then, when people have a shallow, ineffectual experience, we wonder why they no longer want to participate."

Grant Fishbook is following suit. He trumpets the value of the two- or three-person group as a "workable" size that can meet before or even during the workday, not just in the evening, when scheduling conflicts are frequent. He is not working as hard to "squeeze" groups "into a mold." Instead, he is "trying to get them to do the right things." Fishbook participates in a three-person group each Thursday, early in the morning. He is finding that his level of disclosure is much greater than it ever was in a ten-person group: "It feels safer to me." Bill Joy, cofounder of Sun Microsystems, believes the ideal size of a group is "one where people don't have meetings, they have lunch. The size of the meeting should be the size of the lunch table." That ends up being smaller than the average house church or small group.

Then there is the smallest unit yet. An "army of one" is the most indivisible, atomic expression of the church. There has never been a time when the individual can be more empowered for ministry than today. At CTK Durango, church members intentionally join various community groups in order to infiltrate existing social networks with the love of Christ. The impact of even a small church can be greatly expanded when members see themselves as the seeds of a church and launch their own personal ministries within their circles of influence.

The challenge for the megachurch is to tap in to the power of the small. It has already tapped in to the power of the big, but in order to bring about intimacy, the large church must break itself down into subsidiary parts. Thomas likens this practice to children "taming" the ocean by scooping a small hole in the sand near the edge of the sea and creating a "mini-sea" that is manageable.[1] The networked church is the way to continue to grow large while creating a small-church environment. Many large organizations are exploring subsidiarity as a way to make their companies more personal. The W hotels, an up-and-coming boutique chain, work with a "hotel within a hotel" concept. They see personal attention as their secret ingredient. They want to treat people as individuals. To do so, they think of their workers as a cast to inspire a social scene. Their staff members are not there so much to get things done as to be social architects, making connections with patrons.

The innovations in the hotel industry are not unlike innovations that are coming to education. Large high schools are creating "schools within a school." The so-called multiplexes, with five to ten schools within the school, create student communities with specific emphases, such as the arts or community service. The schools share one principal and one set of sport and club offerings but have dedicated staff and teachers. Tom Vander Ark of the Gates Foundation, which is inspiring much of this innovation, says, "Small schools simply produce an environment where it's easier to create a positive climate."[2]

The bigger a church is, the smaller it should act. A key shift in mentality for the megachurch is to see itself in service to the small instead of the other way around. How do small and big relate to each other? Is small in service to the big, or is big in service to the small? What we have tended to see in the church is the small in service to the big. What seems more common in nature is for the big to be in service to the small. A full-grown mother cares for an infant that is 5 percent of her size. And at all levels of nature you see this theme repeated. For instance, in a forest you might find some extremely large trees. But there are some smaller flora and fauna that can survive only in the shade of those trees. So maybe it's not whether it's big or small, but whether the opposite is ultimately valued and protected.

One megachurch that has successfully protected the small is North Point Church, near Atlanta. Hall comments on North Point's approach to moving people toward greater intimacy:

> When it comes to moving people into deeper spiritual waters, North Point Church . . . provides a great example of maximizing the extremities while giving fittingly minimal attention to the middle. They talk about moving people "from the foyer to the kitchen," which roughly means from large scale worship

experiences to small group participation, or from anonymous to intimate. The middle step (I believe they refer to it as "the living room") is an important one-time meeting that helps people consider and get started in a small group. Contrast this with typical Sunday school, a big middle strategy aimed at getting everyone to attend classes that avoid anonymity while rarely developing intimacy.[3]

Kudos to North Point for its emphasis on intimacy. Big churches sometimes don't value these smaller transactions, preferring to put their efforts into the presentational aspect of ministry as a greater return on investment. But almost everything big started out small, including churches. In the case of Lakewood Church, the largest megachurch in America, its leaders talk a lot about the early days, when the congregation met in a small rented storefront and manifested extraordinary faith. Lakewood Church became large because it was powerful when it was small. For large churches desiring to create greater intimacy, a good way to begin is to reminisce about the essence of community that was present in the beginning, and then take people back to that.

Many megachurches are moving toward villagization. Instead of trying to grow larger, they are spawning simpler, smaller, warmer, more intimate ministries. Callahan likens this reverse progression to the process of downsizing one's home:

Some people move into a large house, excited and enthusiastic with all the vast space they now have. But after living there awhile, they discover they are really using only a few rooms in the house. They simply have found they do not need all the space they thought they did. They prefer not to spend their time cleaning space they do not really use. They move to a smaller house.

Some people, as their life circumstances change, move to a smaller house. Their children may be grown and gone, or the activities they now do require less space. They decide to move from the old homestead that had been home for years. It is too big. It is now hard to keep up. Thus they move to a space that matches who they are now.

Some congregations, as their life circumstances change, move to a smaller house. In the heyday of the church's culture of the 1940s and 1950s, some congregations got caught up with the enthusiasm of the times and the building booms all around. Everyone was building. They decided to build too. They overbuilt.[4]

In home construction, there is clearly a trend toward coziness. Even within larger homes, there is renewed emphasis on intimate spaces, such as the kitchen or den. These are the sorts of adjustments you are seeing in both the physical and the social architecture of the church. Large churches are downshifting from sprawling single-use spaces to smaller multiuse spaces.

In order to balance impact with intimacy, in some cases the best strategy for the megachurch is to partner with smaller discipleship groups and house churches in the area. Many microchurch leaders would welcome a conversation initiated by an established pastor in the area, particularly if the pastor's approach was collegial. For megachurch leaders interested in maximum impact, it is really about having enough vision to think small.

The cell opens up "the value of operating in small, dispersed bands as opposed to a concentrated army, keeping in constant motion, never forming a front, flank, or rear for the other side to hit. . . . Done right, guerrilla warfare is virtually unbeatable."[5] This is a great attraction to the aggressive leader if he has enough courage to think bigger than being a great ministry and begin thinking of being a great movement. When we have thought large, we have not thought large enough. We have typically thought of the megachurch of a few thousand. We need to be thinking about how the church can be hundreds of thousands, if not millions. If we link the vision of the mega-church with the scalability of the microchurch, it's possible.

Whereas small churches often aspire to be bigger, and large churches frequently reminisce about the "good ol' days" when they were smaller (and everybody knew everybody), the medium-size church feels tension in both directions. For the church in the middle, the relative merits of size depend on the answers to some other questions.

Are people being treated personally or impersonally? Call me old-fashioned, but it seems that it should be possible for a person to actually get to know other people in the church. I've encountered staff members of large churches who have never met the pastors in the churches in which they serve. The modern world has given us these constructs, but it seems to me that the church of Jesus Christ should be a little more personal than that.

And yet I have also visited very small congregations where no one greeted me, where I felt invisible. In others, there was little concern for how the church could meet the needs of the individual and more concern for how the individual could meet the needs of the church. In one small church my family and I visited in the Midwest, church members escorted us to the nursery, where they proceeded to turn the lights on and told us to make ourselves at home. I guess we were the nursery staff for the day! This church, while homey, was sadly lacking in professionalism.

Whether a church takes a professional approach or not, people need to somehow be engaged in the work. Crowds tend toward people sitting around listening, taking notes, and going home. We don't want this, and we tend to get less of it in smaller congregations. But it is possible for a larger congregation to have high participation in small groups and mitigate this tendency. It is also possible for a small church to be an assemblage of some very self-interested individuals, more like a passive club than an active church.

Self-centeredness can abound regardless of the size of the church. Left to ourselves, we can quickly circle the wagons. We build towers and walls. We look to be blessed instead of being a blessing. Jesus' instructions were clear: Go. As Adam found out, this is not about Eden, this is about filling the Earth with the glory of God. As Abraham found out, this is not about the comfort of the ranch but about following God and seeing all nations on Earth blessed. As the early church found out, this is not about staying in Jerusalem but about going and making disciples of all nations.

The hybrid church may be in the best position to fulfill the great commission. The resources that you need to launch often come out of bigness. The entrepreneurial spirit of adventure often comes out of smallness. Maybe there's a sweet spot here, where we can be big enough to spawn but small enough to do it quickly. There is a tendency, as groups become more established (in either their smallness or their bigness), to not keep moving toward people and instead to try to get people moving toward us. This is not a good development, regardless of whether it's caused by the lethargy of bigness or the comfortableness of smallness.

The Cooperation of Hybrid

The Christian philosopher Francis Schaeffer has said that there are no small churches and no big pastors. Nevertheless, it does take a "big" pastor to cooperate with another pastor, and a "big" church to cooperate with another church (whatever its size) in the building of Christ's kingdom. Some churches will be able to express the best of intimacy and impact in an intrachurch manner. Others will need to link up with other ministries in an interchurch manner.

Shirky suggests a hierarchy of social arrangements—sharing, cooperation, collaboration, and collectivism—that can bring us together.[6] There is increasing coordination with each step. Sharing involves things. Cooperation involves ideas. Collaboration involves projects. And collectivism involves vision. The sequence of these steps is quite logical. But even before you get to the first step, there is a preliminary threshold you must clear: communication. The possibilities of hybridity begin with conversations, with sharing a cup of coffee.

Where the hybrid church is emerging—say, in Los Angeles, Capetown, Austin, or Durango—it is because pastors are spending quality time with each other. A foundation of caring and trust is being laid, on which cooperative efforts can be built. Thinus Coetzee reminds us that intimacy rhymes with "into me see," and he suggests that fellowship can only follow disclosure, and disclosure can only follow humility. Pride is the greatest, and maybe only, obstacle in the way of the interchurch hybrids that are emerging.

Tony Dale acknowledges that many microchurch leaders "don't respond to megachurch leadership." Some have had painful church experiences in the past, from which they are recovering. Many are uncomfortable with hierarchical leadership forms, having built the house church with no control. This aversion to hierarchy is so great that "they do not view the weaknesses that come from lack of control to be great enough to trade for more control."

Megachurch leaders also have been wounded by "friendly fire." As people have left the established church, they haven't always left gracefully. Leaders of large churches may not be as strong as they look. They are real people who get wounded in the fight and have a tendency, after repeatedly being stung, to dismiss the concerns expressed by the microchurch as more of an annoyance than anything else. One megachurch leader quotes John Wayne: "The wagon train doesn't stop for every barking dog." But the analogy breaks down when it is a brother on the side of the road.

Perhaps before cooperation can happen, there needs to be healing from past hurts. We might need to extend forgiveness, let go of our right to be right, and see a bigger puzzle for which we do not have all the pieces. It will no doubt take an act of the Spirit to cause us to admit that there are pieces we don't have instead of promoting the puzzle pieces we've got.

After God has done a work of forgiveness in us, we need to initiate purposeful relationships. Who should initiate this contact? Either. As Bill Hybels says, "Just walk across the room." If you are a small-church leader, get some coffee with the pastor of the big church in town, and vice versa. In fact, even better if vice versa. There is something very beautiful about a large-church pastor being vulnerable with the pastor of a smaller church. When the person in a power position reaches out, it sets in motion a virtuous cycle of community.

One thing is for sure: interdependence is hard, wherever it is attempted. I'm a fan of marriage, but when you think of it, it is a really challenging proposition. Marriage is two people, of different genders, from two different families, trying to do life together as a unit. Good luck with that, especially when visions collide. Everything is cool until the visions vary, and then cool quickly becomes hot. It's a collision course that I'm not sure can be negotiated, at least in our own strength. But God is not beyond asking us to do something that can't be done apart from His help. In the movie *A League of Their Own*, Tom Hanks's character responds to a complaint of hardship by saying, "Hard is what makes it great!" Perhaps the best part of the hybrid church is what God will have to do in us for it to happen.

To validate those whose ministry is different from ours, we need to recognize, rejoice in, and report on what God is doing throughout the world, particularly in ways that are different from what we're used to doing or are doing. His work is much bigger than any of us. Other churches can reach people that your church cannot, and in ways that your church does not. Do I hear an *Amen*? Validate the thing that is different from you, maybe the opposite of you. For those of us in less structured, organic settings, it might mean expressing thanks for the ministries that are programmatic, institutional, or traditional. For those of us in a church that is traditionally organized, it might mean expressing thanks for those who are less structured in their approach.

When was the last time you said to a pastor of another church, "I thank God for what you are doing over there"?

It's time to give a good report about ministries of other styles, in other places. Spread some good gossip. As Ben Franklin said, "Speak ill of no man, but speak all the good you know about everybody." Are you talking up other ministries, or only your own? Grant Fishbook, who pastors the largest CTK Worship Center, likes to talk up the work of one of the smallest CTK centers, in Kendall, Washington. The small group in Kendall has renovated a tavern in its town (formerly the Holy Smoke Tavern) and is now a "city on a hill" that cannot be hidden. Fishbook exclaims, "I think that is so cool!" Those kinds of exclamations wonderfully close the gap between the mega and the micro.

In our CTK services, I like to pray publicly for the other churches in the community. I think it sends an important message that there are other family members around that have valid ministries, even though their perspectives may differ from ours. As I pray for different denominations by name, I can sometimes discern that some of "our" people are squirming. We have done too good a job of differentiating ourselves from other churches, and not a good enough job of communicating our mutual dependence. But this can change. Sheep are prone to follow. And if they have followed us to independence, I believe they will also follow us toward interdependence.

Tony Dale suggests that megachurches and microchurches have ended up in different places because they have been led by different kinds of leaders. "The microchurch has been built on the foundation of pastors and teachers," he says, "while the megachurch has been built upon the foundation of apostles and prophets." See Ephesians 4:11–16:

> It was he who gave some to be apostles, some to be prophets, some to be evangelists, and some to be pastors and teachers, to prepare God's people for works of service, so that the body of

Christ may be built up until we all reach unity in the faith and in the knowledge of the Son of God and become mature, attaining to the whole measure of the fullness of Christ. Then we will no longer be infants, tossed back and forth by the waves, and blown here and there by every wind of teaching and by the cunning and craftiness of men in their deceitful scheming. Instead, speaking the truth in love, we will in all things grow up into him who is the Head, that is, Christ. From him the whole body, joined and held together by every supporting ligament, grows and builds itself up in love, as each part does its work.

The hybrid church seeks to meld these leadership gifts and create more of a well-rounded body. Note that it takes five different gifts to yield one unified body. Any single person who thinks that he or she is bringing to the body everything it needs is not reading clearly. The mutual respect that needs to be developed in the body overall must be exemplified at the leadership level, among the apostles, prophets, evangelists, pastors, and teachers. We need all the leaders in the kingdom working in concert to win the spiritual war.

In conventional war, we see the value of being able to wage both an effective air war and a ground war. Fighter jets overhead give needed cover for boots on the ground. Yet foot soldiers are needed to secure gains won from the air. The air force and the army need each other to win the war. Neither can say, "I don't need you." The slogan we need for the church in America is the one printed on our money: *E pluribus unum* (out of many, one). At times in the church, there has been too much *pluribus* and not enough *unum*. Of course, the Lord's Prayer (not the one He taught us to pray, but the one He actually prayed) was for unity. As Christ is praying for unity, there is also an enemy roaming who is intent on division.

C. S. Lewis, in *The Great Divorce*, illustrates this point as he recounts a bus ride from heaven to hell. Instead of finding fire in hell, he finds a neighborhood full of empty homes on deserted streets. Lewis asks what has happened, and he gets a chilling answer. There used to be a great population in hell, he is told, but on the first day when someone would arrive, he would start quarreling with his neighbor, and within a week he would move to another block. Of course, someone else would move in next to him in that neighborhood as well. So the person would have to move again to get away from his neighbors. This cycle was repeated many times, until the person had moved to the edge of town, where he had to build another house. And that was hell—a constant drive to get away from others. Hell meant growing—rapidly—apart.[7] That is a metaphor for hell on earth, and also an indicator of what heaven on earth must be like: coming together.

The Creativity of Hybrid

If you come over to my house sometime, I'll offer you my concoction. That's the best I can do to describe it. My concoction is a drink that I make in a coffee cup. It combines one and a half scoops of vanilla espresso mix with three-quarters of a scoop of frozen chocolate mocha mix and 190-degree hot water. The taste is a swirl of vanilla, chocolate, and espresso. It ends up being a delightful drink on some of the wet, cold nights we enjoy in Washington State. I've thought of giving it a cool name like "vanilla-chino" or "chocovano" (maybe I should go to work for Starbucks), but so far I've just called it my concoction. I started making the concoction by accident. I ran out of vanilla espresso mix and had to supplement with the chocolate mocha mix. Since then I've tweaked the mixture several times, adjusting the ratio in one direction or the other. But I knew I had arrived when I had a distinct taste of both chocolate and vanilla. That is the creative tension of hybrid.

I was recently at a multisite conference where I was one of three pastors who told our stories. We were each chosen because we represented slightly different approaches to being one church in many locations. Backstage, prior to one of the sessions, some-one commented on how cool it was that three different churches with three different styles could come together at one confer-ence. I jokingly quipped, "But aren't we really here to find out which approach is right?" There was nervous laughter because we all knew that much of sordid church history has been the quest to find the one "right" way.

It's about time we realize that there is not *a* right way. There are just right *ways*. There is no perfect hybrid. Hybrid churches come in different shapes and sizes. Churches are like finger-prints. There are no two exactly alike. The key is to become the best you that you can be. It's about choosing the model that maximizes opportunities in your context. The sweet spot may vary from ministry to ministry.

The term *sweet spot* is used to express the place of ultimate effect. When a golfer strikes a ball with the sweet spot of the club, he gets the greatest possible power and control from the impact. The key is to get both of those from *one swing*. If a golfer only wants to hit an accurate shot, he will care more about the point of contact between the club face and the ball. If his objective is distance, then the concern shifts to the power and velocity with which the club strikes the ball. The great ones have to be able to hit it hard while hitting it well. In a similar manner, the great churches will be powerful yet personal.

Finding the sweet spot between intimacy and impact may be an act of creativity. God is not formulaic in His approach. Craig Groeschel, a megachurch pastor, says, "In order to reach people that no one is reaching, you may have to do things that no one is doing. In order to do things that no one else is doing, you can't do what everyone else is doing." One of the reasons we have so many differences in the body of Christ is that God's ways (plural, remember?) are personal and pro-found, mysterious and multifaceted. Just when we think we have Him figured out, the pillar of fire and cloud moves. The sooner we get our heads around *ways* instead of *way*, the more enjoyment we will find in the way that God is at work in our own and others' ministries.

Joseph and Moses had very similar experiences, with very different conclusions. They both were raised in Egyptian royal households. They both rose to positions of prominence and had potential for significant power. But in Joseph's case, the power was part of the plan that God had for him, whereas Moses needed to shun that power to follow God's script. It's a good thing they followed what God had in mind for them and didn't copy what they had read in a Christian magazine. Just because God is at work in a certain way in someone's else's story doesn't mean He wants to work that way in yours.

In early 2009, a GM executive declared, "We think a plug-in offering forty miles of gas- and emissions-free driving like the Volt is the sweet spot for the majority of customers." Will there be people who will not purchase the Volt because it has a range of only forty miles? Yes. Will GM provide the option of a gasoline engine to extend the range? Yes. Will there be a market for an electric vehicle? It appears so. But when it comes to blending economy and performance, there are multiple possibilities and uncertainties.

In the area of print media, there is a new blurring of text, audio, and video with e-readers such as Amazon's Kindle and Apple's iPad. Multidimensional delivery is expected to become commonplace. John Yoo, David Levithan, and Rachel Griffiths created a children's series called *The 39 Clues*. The series is a book/Internet hybrid where readers find ten of the clues in the book and the other twenty-nine through a Web site. The first three books sold more than two and a half million copies. Levithan says that kids deal quite well with the virtual version of the physical book, tending not to make a strong distinction between the version of the story they read in the book and the version they experience online. This development forecasts shifts that are coming in all printed materials (with digital e-readers like the Kindle or the iPad providing interactivity) but may also signal shifts in delivery of ministry. Perhaps instead of delivering ministry in one or two dimensions (say, by offering a class on marriage), new ministry forms will include a blend of blog, book, mentorship, retreat, classroom, and rally. It will probably take a while for the church to realize the possibilities. Could megachurch pastors teach on a topic that smaller house fellowships would then develop in depth? Could the needs that surface in house churches inform the programming of the megachurch?

Thompson, writing about new short-form video possibilities (like YouTube), says, "Whenever we get our hands on a new medium, we tend to use it like older ones. Early TV broadcasts consisted of guys sitting around reading radio scripts because nobody had realized yet that TV could tell stories differently. It's the same with much of today's webcam video; most people still try to emulate TV and film."[8]

Among the first generation of people who grew up online (the so-called digital natives, people between the ages of eighteen and thirty-four), TV viewership has dropped for the first time in fifty years. People in this age group are still glued to a screen, but it's not necessarily a TV screen. The audience has migrated from broadcast TV to the Internet and now the cell phone, where niche economies rule. Quantifying viewership becomes much more difficult when programming formats are diverse and programs are consumed à la carte. The next challenge for industry executives is to quantify the cumulative number of people reached through broadcast, streaming, and downloads. Perhaps a day is coming when church attendance includes those who are downloading sermons as well as listening to them live, or those who are meeting in coffee shops on Saturday morning as well as those in attendance in the auditorium.

At CTK, we do not expect every small group or Worship Center to look exactly the same. Some people will have very high participation in midweek small groups, and others will be more oriented around the weekend worship service. There will be similarity in principles but differences in style and personality. This is normal and natural. As the saying goes, "There are no two snowflakes alike." It behooves us to appreciate the remarkable variety that can be found.

In organic life, repetition and revelation are constants. I have often said, "If you've seen one CTK Worship Center, you've seen one CTK Worship Center." As I have visited CTK Centers around the world, I always come away with two feelings: first, that this is CTK; and, second, that I've never seen anything quite like this before. But I think the same thing about each of my children, too. Each of them has two arms, two legs, and one nose. It is even clear that they share the same parents. But that is where the similarities end and differences begin. Each of them is very individual, a real revelation.

At CTK, we are not attempting cloning. We are trying to build an ever-expanding family of relationships. We want to be more like a family than a factory, more like a forest than a tree farm. In a tree farm, trees are planted in rows and groomed so they look self-similar. In a forest, a remarkable variety exists of big, small, straight, and crooked. When you get back far enough from a forest, you see a pattern. But upon closer inspection, you observe immense variation.

In the CTK story, our mission, vision, and values (our core DNA) get worked out with varied emphasis. I saw this clearly when I took recent trips to Africa and India. Both are Third World regions, and CTK has expanded rapidly in both places, with hundreds of new leaders. Both movements manifest CTK's commitment to the priorities of worship, small groups, and outreach. But they do so in varying ways.

In Africa, the dominant trait is small groups. We have always contended that small groups are the primary convention for the people of CTK, but in Africa they have taken this ideal to another level. As best we can tell, there are 862 house fellowships throughout the continent. In some communities, there are five to ten small groups meeting, and they have yet to have a public (temple courts) meeting because they are so intensely focused on the value of community, with small groups being the basic building block.

In India, the dominant trait is outreach. We have always contended that we need to keep the arrows pointed out—that it is not our goal to get everyone to come to us, but to get us to go to them. In India, CTK evangelists have visited more than a thousand villages, many where the Gospel of Christ had never been preached before. Circuit riding is common. Lay evangelists are prominent. From district to district, they are establishing Worship Centers. They are taking "arrows out" to a new level.

A great mistake, in my opinion, would be to try to get the African groups to behave more like the Indian groups, and vice versa. That would be a typical, top-down, organizational response. As members of organizations, we have been trained to look for differences and eliminate them. I wouldn't advise you as a parent to remove all the variations you see among your kids. And the same advice applies to spiritual parents with their spiritual offspring.

There are management challenges, of course, as the possibilities become more divergent. Xenos Christian Fellowship has been experiencing tension over the varying levels of engagement in its house churches, particularly among middle-aged people with children, whose family obligations create severe time conflicts. The church recently rolled out the idea that groups can charter themselves by saying, in effect, "This is what we'll do together." There will be some groups with higher discipline and some with lesser. Some will meet more frequently, and some will meet less frequently. Some will be organized for hardcore discipleship, and some will be loosely structured for fellowship. Then the church will let people go where they want to go. It appears that people are going to have to find their way in the hybrid church, just as the leaders are doing.

Barna has become a proponent of the microchurch and the "mini-movements" being inspired by them, but he points out that "there is a pervasive mindset . . . that all legitimate spiritual activity must flow through a local church." He notes that even very large parachurch organizations that relate to tens of millions of people around the world view their work as "second fiddle" to the ministry of the local church. Barna's response is to say, "Whether religious leaders deem it appropriate or not, God is facilitating incredible transformation in the minds and hearts of millions of people involved with the mini-movements."[9]

The hybrid world in which we live calls for a new ecclesiology that is not bound by denominations, buildings, or budgets but by the life-changing, life-giving work of the Holy Spirit. Cole likes to speak of the church as a spiritual family.[10] The metaphor of family speaks to relationship more than to rules and regulations.

Tony Dale spends all week involved in kingdom work. He has several Christian fellowships to which he belongs, including his Sunday night house church. He has trained more than 350 leaders over the years and is in weekly contact with many of them. He is heavily involved in the incipient megachurch-microchurch conversation. But because he is not tied in to a traditional Sunday morning church, he chuckles, "It's kind of bizarre, but what do I do for church?" Only a traditionalist would think that Dale is anything but a fully functioning member of the body of Christ. The church should be defined as all of the ministries that God is undertaking in the relationships between believers, and between believers and the outside world.

Jesus argued for a theology of the church that includes "new wineskins." New wineskins are by definition not the same as the old ones. So get ready. It appears that the change that is coming is a fusion of intimacy and impact.

Notes

Preface

1. G. K. Chesterton, *The Everlasting Man* (Redford, Va.: Wilder Publications, 2008), p. 39.

Introduction

1. Carl F. George, *Prepare Your Church for the Future* (Grand Rapids, Mich.: Fleming H. Revell, 1992).
2. Barna Research, "House Church Involvement Is Growing" (http://www.barna.org/barna-update/article/19-organic-church/151-house-church-involvement-is-growing), June 19, 2006.
3. Pew Research Center, "Many Americans Mix Multiple Faiths" (http://pewforum.org/docs/?DocID=490), December 9, 2009.
4. Lillian Kwon, "US Megachurches Growing—and Fast" (http://www.christiantoday.com/article/us.megachurches.growing.and.fast/21421.htm), September 14, 2008.
5. G. K. Chesterton, *Orthodoxy* (Teddington, Middlesex, England: Echo Library, 2006), p. 41.
6. Clayton M. Christensen, *The Innovator's Dilemma: When New Technologies Cause Great Firms to Fail* (Boston: Harvard Business Press, 1997).
7. Tom Peters, *Re-imagine: Business Excellence in a Disruptive Age* (London: Dorling Kindersley, 2003), p. 237.

8. G. K. Chesterton, *Orthodoxy*, p. 223.

9. Richard Bliese, "A Small Church Redefines Its Mission," *The Christian Century*, July 12, 2003, p. 26.

10. Scott Thumma and Dave Travis, *Beyond Megachurch Myths: What We Can Learn from America's Largest Churches* (San Francisco: Jossey-Bass, 2007).

11. Carlos Whittaker, "Mega-Church Myths" (http://www.ragamuffinsoul.com/2008/08/mega-church-myths), August 6, 2008.

12. Christian A. Schwarz, *Natural Church Development: A Guide to Eight Essential Qualities of Healthy Churches* (Saint Charles, Ill.: ChurchSmart Resources, 1996), p. 48.

13. G. K. Chesterton, *The Everlasting Man* (Redford, Va.: Wilder Publications, 2008), p. 39.

14. Max Lucado, *Cure for the Common Life* (Nashville: Thomas Nelson, 2005), p. 116.

15. Huston Smith, *The World's Religions: Our Great Wisdom Traditions* (New York: HarperCollins, 1991), p. 292.

16. G. K. Chesterton, *Orthodoxy*, p. 104.

17. George, *Prepare Your Church for the Future*.

18. Hannah Holmes, *Suburban Safari: A Year on the Lawn* (New York: Bloomsbury, 2005).

Chapter 1: The Extreme World

1. Daniel Pink, "The Shape of Things to Come," *Wired*, May 2003, p. 23.

2. Leonard Sweet, *The Gospel According to Starbucks: Living with a Grande Passion* (Colorado Springs: WaterBrook Multnomah, 2007).

3. Chad Hall, "Leader's Insight: The Disappearing Middle" (http://www.christianitytoday.com/le/currenttrendscolumns/leadershipweekly/cln70716.html), July 16, 2007.

4. Steven Johnson, "Snacklash: In Praise of the Full Meal," *Wired*, March 2007, p. 178.

5. G. K. Chesterton, *Orthodoxy* (Teddington, Middlesex, England: Echo Library, 2006), p. 62.
6. Jeff Jarvis, cited in Clive Thompson, "The BitTorrent Effect," *Wired*, January 2005, p. 178.
7. Thomas Friedman, cited in Daniel Pink, "Why the World Is Flat," *Wired*, May 2005, p. 152.
8. Sweet, *The Gospel According to Starbucks*, p. 40.

Chapter 2: The Fallacy of Either/Or

1. Jim Collins, cited in Joe Flower, "Building a Visionary Organization Is a Do-It-Yourself Project: An Interview with Jim Collins," *Healthcare Forum Journal*, September 1995.
2. Tom Rath, *Vital Friends: The People You Can't Afford to Live Without* (New York: Gallup, 2006).
3. Seth Godin, *Small Is the New Big and 183 Other Riffs, Rants, and Remarkable Business Ideas* (New York: Penguin, 2006), pp. 216–17.
4. Chris Anderson, *The Long Tail* (New York: Hyperion, 2006).
5. David Lascelles, cited by Tom Peters, Seminar2000 (www.tompeters.com/slides/uploaded/copenhagen.ppt), Copenhagen, Denmark, December 13, 2000.
6. G. K. Chesterton, *The Outline of Sanity* (San Francisco: Ignatius, 1987), p. 86.
7. Chris Anderson, "The Rise and Fall of the Hit," *Wired*, July 2006, p. 39.
8. Seth Godin, *Purple Cow* (New York: Penguin, 2003), p. 5.
9. Gary L. McIntosh, *One Size Doesn't Fit All: Bringing Out the Best in Any Size Church* (Ada, Mich.: Fleming H. Revell, 1999).
10. Jim Collins, *Good to Great: Why Some Companies Make the Leap . . . and Others Don't* (New York: HarperCollins, 2001), p. 121.
11. Hartford Institute, "New Research Shows Megachurches Growing in Influence" (http://hirr.hartsem.edu/megachurch/megastoday2008_pressrelease.html), September 12, 2008.

12. William C. Symonds, "Earthly Empires," *Newsweek*, May 23, 2005.
13. Mark Galli, *Jesus Mean and Wild: The Unexpected Love of an Untamable God* (Ada, Mich.: Baker Books, 2008).
14. Tom Peters, *Re-imagine: Business Excellence in a Disruptive Age* (London: Dorling Kindersley, 2003), p. 143.
15. Eric Bonabeau, Marco Dorigo, and Guy Theraulaz, *Swarm Intelligence: From Natural to Artificial Systems* (New York: Oxford University Press, 1999).
16. Godin, *Small Is the New Big*, p. 217.
17. Anderson, *The Long Tail*, p. 167.
18. Malcolm Gladwell, *The Tipping Point: How Little Things Can Make a Big Difference* (Boston: Back Bay Books, 2000), p. 182.
19. Godin, *Small Is the New Big*, pp. 217–218.
20. Mark Ward, *Beyond Chaos: The Underlying Theory Behind Life, the Universe, and Everything* (New York: Thomas Dunne, 2001), p. 85.

Chapter 3: The Beauty of Both/And

1. Canabou, Christine. "Free to Innovate," *Fast Company*, October 31, 2001, p. 60.
2. Mark Buchanan, *The Rest of God: Restoring Your Soul by Restoring Sabbath* (Nashville: Thomas Nelson, 2006), p. 119.

Chapter 4: The Emerging Blends

1. Neil Cole, *Search and Rescue: Becoming a Disciple Who Makes a Difference* (Grand Rapids, Mich.: Baker, 2008), p. 230.
2. Fraser Morrison, cited in Larry Ferrell, *The Entrepreneurial Age* (New York: Allworth, 2000), p. 305.

Chapter 5: The Convergence of Intimacy and Impact

1. Gary Thomas, *Sacred Pathways: Discover Your Soul's Path to God* (Grand Rapids, Mich.: Zondervan, 2010).

2. Tom Vander Arkm, cited in Linda Shaw, "Schools' New Motto: Think Small," *Seattle Times*, December 3, 2003, p. A13.

3. Chad Hall, "Leader's Insight: The Disappearing Middle" (http://www.christianitytoday.com/le/currenttrendscolumns/leadershipweekly/cln70716.html), July 16, 2007.

4. Kennon Callahan, *Strong, Small Congregations: Creating Strengths and Health for Your Congregation* (San Francisco: Jossey-Bass, 2000), p. 253.

5. Robert Greene, *The 33 Strategies of War* (New York: Viking, 2006), p. 349.

6. Clay Shirky, *Here Comes Everybody: The Power of Organizing Without Organizations* (New York: Penguin, 2008).

7. C. S. Lewis, *The Great Divorce* (New York: Macmillan, 1977).

8. Clive Thompson, "The BitTorrent Effect," *Wired*, January 2005, p. 177.

9. George Barna, *Revolution* (Carol Stream, Ill.: Tyndale House, 2005), p. 55.

10. Neil Cole, *Search and Rescue: Becoming a Disciple Who Makes a Difference* (Grand Rapids, Mich.: Baker, 2008).

The Author

Dave Browning is a visionary minimalist and the founder of Christ the King Community Church, International (CTK). CTK is a nondenominational multilocation church that has been noted as one of the fastest-growing and most innovative churches in America, thanks to its employment of the K.I.S.S. (Keep It Simple and Scalable) method.

Dave's vision for CTK is to see a prevailing multilocation church emerge that will transform the spiritual landscape. This church will convene in hundreds of small groups, with Worship Centers strategically located in every community. Since its beginning in 1999, CTK has become a minimovement, with locations in a number of states and countries.

Before joining CTK, Dave pastored in traditional and megachurch contexts. His experiences have led him to write about the church as a hybrid of intimacy and impact. Dave's previous books are *Deliberate Simplicity: How the Church Does More by Doing Less* (2009), *What Leaders Do: A Leadership Primer* (2009), and *Welcome Home . . . to the God Who Loves You* (2008).

Dave and his wife, Kristyn, have three children—Erika, Jenna, and Daron—and live in Burlington, Washington.

Index

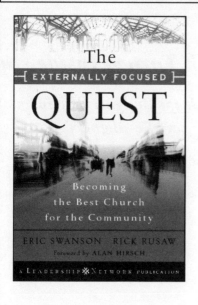

The Externally Focused Quest

Becoming the Best Church for the Community

Eric Swanson | Rick Rusaw

ISBN: 978-0-470-50078-1

Hardback | 272 pp.

"Swanson and Rusaw are unmatched in their grasp of church and culture! This book contains the information and insight that will resource my preaching, refine my strategy, and reignite my passion as a pastor."

—Dr. Joel C. Hunter, senior pastor, Northland – A Church Distributed, Longwood, Florida

A practical approach for leaders to guide their congregations to become more externally focused.

The Externally Focused Quest is designed for church leaders who want to transform their churches to become less internally focused and more oriented to the world around them. The book includes the clear guidelines on the ten changes congregations must adopt to become truly outwardly focused. This book is not about getting all churches to have an annual day of community service as a tactic but changing the core of who they are and how they see themselves as a part of their community.

This book reveals what it takes to make the major shift from an internal to external focus and how that affects church leadership.

Other Books of Interest

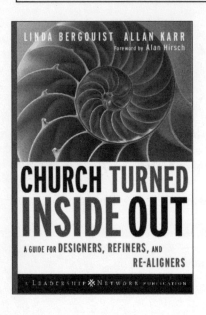

Church Turned Inside Out

A Guide for Designers, Refiners, and Re-Aligners

Linda Bergquist | Allan Karr

ISBN: 978-0-470-38317-9

Hardback | 240 pp.

"What an extremely hopeful, heart-lifting, and practical book for anyone who loves the church. We must never be afraid to look at our church from the inside out as that is where true change will happen."

—Dan Kimball author, *They Like Jesus but Not the Church*

A practical, creative guide for planting or redesigning a church and developing leaders.

Written by Linda Bergquist and Allan Karr, two experienced church planters and mentors/teachers, *Church Turned Inside Out* offers church leaders a new way to think about how their churches are run. Taking cues from the world of business and offering a multi-disciplined and leading-edge approach, the authors stress the importance of incorporating the design process when establishing a new church or planning the ongoing future of an established church. This groundbreaking book also includes ideas for becoming a more effective church leader.

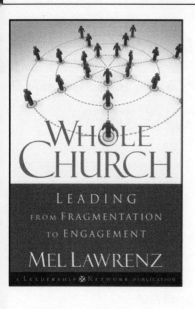

Whole Church

Leading from Fragmentation to Engagement

Mel Lawrenz

ISBN: 978-0-470-25934-4

Hardback | 208 pp.

"Mel is a thoughtful analyst of church life today. Best of all—he actually does what he writes about. This book can lead to new levels of engagement for your church."

—John Ortberg, author and pastor, Menlo Park Presbyterian Church

"Wow! This book is for every Christian leader who wants to move their church from a narrow self-focus to active engagement in the world with all the resources and possibilities of heaven."

—Mike Slaughter, Ginghamsburg Church

A new model for creating greater involvement and cohesion in churches.

Mel Lawrenz has been using an engaged, "whole church/whole-ministry" value system, strategy, and commitment in his missional church. He provides a new model to help churches maximize their strengths and revitalize their ministries through engaging with God, each other, their community, and the world. This "engagement" model is not merely a list of functions or stages of growth–it integrates the church, connecting worship and mission, local witness and global involvement, small groups and personal devotion.

Other Books of Interest

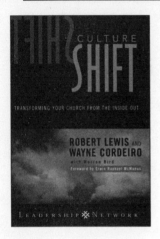

Culture Shift

Transforming Your Church from the Inside Ou

Robert Lewis | Wayne Cordeiro | Warren Bird

ISBN: 978-0-7879-7530-2

Hardback | 256 pp.

"Like snowflakes and fingerprints, every church's culture is unique. Learning the art of cultural analysis and cultural formation shown in Culture Shift *is indispensable for church leaders."*

—John Ortberg, author, *If You Want to Walk on Water* and *The Life You've Always Wanted.*

Culture Shift, written for church leaders, ministers, pastors, ministry teams, and lay leaders, leads you through the process of identifying your church's distinctive culture, gives you practical tools to change it from the inside-out, and provides steps to keep your new culture aligned with your church's mission. Real transformation is not about working harder at what you're already doing or even copying another church's approach but about changing church culture at a foundational level.

The good news is that you already have everything you need— but you must look within for radical, transformational power. Your job is to develop a healthy atmosphere and let the Holy Spirit do the work through you. Once this fundamental shift has occurred and the new habits and values become central to everything your church does, a healthy, energetic, God-honoring church will be unleashed into a world that is desperately crying out for it.